AL-BAYHAQI (D. 458)

ALLAH'S  NAMES AND ATTRIBUTES

(AL-ASMÂ' WA AL-SIFÂT)

EXCERPTS

Translation and Notes by
Gibril Fouad Haddad

Damascus
1998

بسم الله الرّحمن الرّحيم

وصلّى الله على سيّدنا محمّد وعلى آله وصحبه وسلّم

ربّ يسّر ولا تعسّر

This work is humbly dedicated to

Mawlana al-Shaykh Muhammad Nazim Adil al-Qubrusi al-Naqshbandi al-Haqqani,

to Shaykh Muhammad Hisham Kabbani,
and to their friends and followers worldwide.

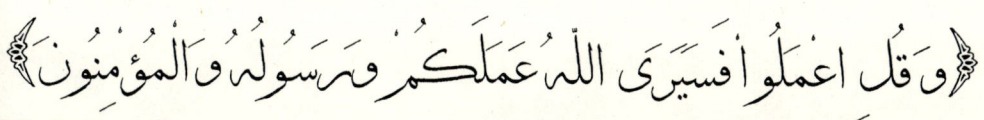

"There are, concerning the hadiths and verses of the divine Attributes, two well-known schools of thought. The school of the vast majority of the *Salaf* and some of the sholars of *kalâm* holds that we must believe in their reality according to what befits Allah, but that the literal import we commonly apply to ourselves is not meant, nor do we say anything to interpret them figuratively, believing firmly that Allah is utterly transcendent above the properties of contingence *(hudûth)*. The second school is that of the majority of the scholars of *kalâm* and a number of the *Salaf* and holds that they are interpreted figuratively but only according to their appropriate contextual meanings." IMAM AL-NAWAWI, *SHARH SAHIH MUSLIM*.

© 1999 As-Sunna Foundation of America

As-Sunna Foundation of America is an affiliate of the Islamic Supreme Council of America. The Islamic Supreme Council of America is a non-profit, non-governmental organization dedicated to working for the cause of Islam on a bilateral level. As an affiliate of ISCA, ASFA strives to promote unity among Muslims and understanding and awareness about mainstream Islam through education. Its focus is on publishing works that support traditional, accepted approaches to Islamic jurisprudence and law.

All rights reserved. No part of this book may be reproduced or utilized in any form or by any means, electronic or mechanical, including photocopying and recording or by any information storage or retrieval system, without the written permission of the publisher. All inquiries may be sent directly to the publisher.

ISBN: 95-930409-03-6

Published by:
As-Sunna Foundation of America
2415 Owen Rd Ste B
Fenton, MI 48430
email: asfa@sunnah.org

www.sunnah.org
www.islamicsupremecouncil.org

Foreword

Bismillahir-Rahmanir-Raheem

All praise is due to Allah Almighty who has revived in the hearts of His servants thirst for understanding the Islamic doctrine, *al-'aqeedah*. Blessings and salutations on His Beloved Servant Muhammad ﷺ, whom He raised to the station of nearness and whom he blessed with the revelation of Divine Guidance.

As-Sunna Foundation of America is honored to make available to the reading public this new set of translations of classical Islamic texts – the *Islamic Doctrines and Beliefs* series. We congratulate Dr. Gabriel Haddad for his efforts in bringing these outstanding classical manuscripts to light in the English language, as these books are a necessity for every Muslim home, school, library and university.

These works have reached us through distant centuries, authored by scholars who spent the whole of their lives in devotion to Allah and to spreading the knowledge of His great religion. They will undoubtedly stand witness for their authors on the Day of Judgment, wherein *"Whoever works righteousness benefits his own soul"* [41: 46], for every drop of blood running in the veins of such pious and sincere sages was infused with their intense devotion to preserve the fundamentals and the branches of Islam. Reliance on classical texts such as this one by Imam al-Bayhaqi leaves little room for the introduction of alien creeds or uneducated speculation. Due to the extravagant efforts scholars made to compile these books, they are comprehensible and applicable to the general reader and student of religion.

Likewise the efforts of Dr. Haddad, who spent long days and nights in perfecting these translations, is something that we pray will be highly rewarded in this life and the next, for his intention and ours is to broadcast and clarify the pure and unadulterated teachings of *Ahl as-Sunna wal-Jama'a,* The People of the Sunnah and the Majority, whose foundations were laid by the Prophet ﷺ under the direction of his Lord, whose walls were erected by the *Salaf as-saliheen*, the pious predecessors, and whose roof and domes were built by the *Khalaf as-sadiqeen*, the truthful successors up to the present age.

The Importance of Knowledge of Correct *'Aqeedah*

Due to the fact that every generation witnesses a silent decline in worshippers' knowledge of the fundamental doctrines and beliefs of religion, constant efforts are required to elucidate and preserve the sources of this knowledge and to preserve them in the hearts and minds of Allah's servants. The acquisition of knowledge is obligatory for every accountable Muslim, for without it the appearance of conjecture and uneducated opinion is inevitable. Therein lies a danger that leads to an erroneous understanding of faith, which if left unchecked, may lead the seeker to a dangerous precipice from which he is unable to escape a serious fall.

There is no time better than today to introduce these books to those for whom English is the mother tongue, for the subject of *'aqeedah* has become one of controversy and confusion. These books provide a classical approach to understanding Islamic doctrine, based on some of the most accepted and reliable scholars of *Ahl as-Sunnah wal-Jama'ah*, the Saved Group.

Knowledge of the Divine Attributes

The correct understanding of the signs of Allah Almighty, His Angels, His Books, His Prophets, the Day of Judgment, and the Divine Decree saves one from two extremes: denial of Allah's attributes, and its opposite anthropomorphism, the relating of Allah's attributes to physical manifestations. Allah is One, Unique – not a body possessing form, nor a substance restricted and limited. Nothing precedes Him; He is without any beginning. He is Eternal with none after Him, Everlasting without any end, subsisting without cessation, abiding without termination He has not ceased and He will not cease to be described by the epithets of Majesty. At the end of time He will not be subject to dissolution and decay, but He is the First and the Last, the Hidden and Apparent, and He knows everything. Such an initial glimpse gives understanding and precision in describing the Names and Attributes of our Lord the Exalted and Majestic. With such understanding comes true acceptance of our limited nature and our absolute abjectness before Him in whose Hands lies our souls and our destiny.

This book, authored by one of the greatest hadith masters, Imam al-Bayhaqi, attempts to bring to light the authentic teachings of *Ahl as-Sunna wal-Jama'a* regarding the Names and Attributes of Allah, Glorified and Exalted. As an Ash'ari and a Shafi'i, al-Bayhaqi followed the mainstream of Islam in both *'aqeedah* (doctrine) and in *fiqh* (jurisprudence). Therefore this classic text is seen as one which elucidates the mainstream viewpoint, illuminating its many fine points and subtleties in language which the average reader and student may grasp. Neither too technical nor too basic, this book treads the fine line between scholarly and commonplace.

Praise be to Allah, Lord of the Worlds, and salutations and blessings of peace on His Perfect Servant, Muhammad ﷺ.

Shaykh Muhammad Hisham Kabbani
1 Ramadan, 1420
December 8, 1999
Fenton, Michigan, USA

Contents

Imam al-Bayhaqi and the Ash'ari School 3
Al-Bayhaqi 3
Imam Abu al-Hasan al-Ash'ari 9
The Prophetic Narrations in Praise of the Ash'aris 15
The Ash'ari School From the Time of al-Ash'ari 17
Al-Ash'ari's Refutation of the *Hashwiyya* and *Mu'tazila* 18
Ibn Mahdi al-Tabari (d. ~380) 21
Al-Khattabi (d. 388) 22
Al-Halimi (d. 403) 23
Al-Hâkim (d. 405) 24
Ibn Furak (d. 406) 26

Allah's Names And Attributes 29
What Allah Is Not 29
The Self-Exalted *(al-Muta'âl)* 29
The Most Hidden *(al-Bâtin)* 30
The All-Hearing *(al-Samî')* 30
The All-Seeing *(al-Basîr)* 30
The Witness *(Al-Shahîd)* 30
Allah's "Nearness" And His "Cover" 31
The Unity Of *Tawhîd* 31
Allah's Speech 32
The Recitation Of The Qur'an 32
Allah's Self *(Nafs)* 34
Allah's Form *(Sûra)* 35
Allah's Hand, Palm, Fingers, etc. 36
The Method In Interpreting The Attributes 38
The Beginning of Creation 39
Allah's Establishment Over The Throne *(Istiwâ')* 39
Allah's Coming *(Ityân)* And Arrival *(Majî')* 43
Allah's Descent *(Nuzûl)* 44
Allah's Facing Of The Worshipper 45
Allah's Face *(Wajh)* 45
Allah's Astonishment *('Ajab)* And Laughter *(Dahik)* 47
Allah's Love *(mahabba)*, Hate *(bughd)*, and Dislike *(karâhiyya)* 47

Appendices 55

1. Allah's Beautiful Names 55
2. The Controversy Over the Pronunciation of the Qur'an 59
3. The Vision of Allah in the World and the Hereafter 71
4. Allah's "Hand" 81
5. *Istiwâ'* Is A Divine Act 87
6. Allah's "Coming" And "Arrival" 95
7. Allah's "Descent" 99
   - Ibn Hajar's Commentary 101
   - Some Misleading Reports From the *Salaf* 104
   - Al-Khattabi's Commentary 105
   - Al-Maturidi, Ibn Hazm, and Ibn 'Abd al-Wahhab 107
   - Ibn 'Abd al-Barr's Controversy 108
   - Ibn al-'Arabi's Refutation of Ibn 'Abd al-Barr 109
   - Al-'Iraqi and Ibn Jahbal's Dismissal of Ibn 'Abd al-Barr 113
   - Al-Qari's Recapitulation 114

Bibliography 121

Imam al-Bayhaqi and the Ash'ari School[1]

Al-Bayhaqi (384-458)

Ahmad ibn al-Husayn ibn 'Ali ibn 'Abd Allah ibn Musa, Abu Bakr al-Bayhaqi al-Naysaburi al-Khusrawjirdi al-Shafi'i al-Ash'ari (384-458), "the jurisprudent imam, hadith master, authority in the foundations of doctrine *(usûli)*, scrupulous and devoted ascetic, defender of the School both in its foundations and its branches, one of the mountains of Islamic knowledge." He is known in the books of the scholars of Naysabur and his direct students as "*al-faqîh* Ahmad." He took *fiqh* from the imam Abu al-Fath Nasir ibn al-Husayn ibn Muhammad al-Qurashi al-'Umari al-Marwazi al-Shafi'i al-Naysaburi (d. 444) among others.

Al-Bayhaqi belongs to the third generation of Imam Abu al-Hasan al-Ash'ari's students and took *kalâm* from the two Ash'ari imams Ibn Furak and Abu Mansur al-Baghdadi. His oldest shaykh was the imam and hadith scholar of Khurasan al-Sayyid Abu al-Hasan Muhammad ibn al-Husayn ibn Dawud al-'Alawi al-Hasani al-Naysaburi al-Hasib (d. 401), who was also the shaykh of the hadith master al-Hakim al-Naysaburi. Al-Bayhaqi's other shaykhs in hadith include the latter, whose foremost pupil he was; the hadith master Abu 'Ali al-Husayn ibn Muhammad ibn Muhammad al-Rudhabari al-Tusi (d. 403);[2] the Ash'ari imam in the foundations of doctrine Abu Bakr ibn Furak (d. 406); the imam, jurist, philologist, and hadith master of Khurasan Abu Tahir Muhammad ibn Muhammad ibn Mahmish al-Ziyadi al-Shafi'i al-Naysaburi (d. 410); the Sufi master, Ash'ari imam, hadith master, and author of *Tabaqat al-Sufiyya* Muhammad ibn al-Husayn ibn Muhammad, Abu 'Abd al-Rahman al-Azdi al-Sulami (d. 411); Muhammad ibn Hibat Allah al-Lalika'i's teacher, Muhammad ibn al-Husayn ibn Muhammad ibn al-Fadl al-Qattan al-Baghdadi (d. 415); and the Ash'ari imam, jurist, and heresiologist Abu Mansur 'Abd al-Qahir al-Baghdadi al-Shafi'i (d. 429).

---

[1] From Ibn al-Subki, *Tabaqat al-Shafi'iyya al-Kubra* (4:8-15 #251), al-Dhahabi, *Siyar A'lam al-Nubala'* (13:529-533 #4159), and Ibn 'Asakir, *Tabyin Kadhib al-Muftari* (p. 260-262).
[2] This is not the Sufi master Abu 'Ali Ahmad ibn Muhammad ibn al-Qasim al-Rudhabari (d. 322).

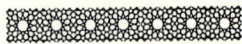 Al-Bayhaqi and the Ash'ari School

It is noteworthy that neither al-Tirmidhi's *Sunan,* nor al-Nasa'i's, nor Ibn Majah's were transmitted to al-Bayhaqi, as stated by al-Dhahabi and others. Al-Dhahabi said: "His sphere in hadith is not large, but Allah blessed him in his narrations for the excellence of his method in them and his sagacity and expertise in the subject-matters and narrators."³

Al-Bayhaqi lived frugally in the manner of the pious scholars. He began fasting perpetually thirty years before his death. Perpetual fast *(sawm al-dahr)* is the practice of several of the Companions and *Salaf* ﷺ such as Ibn 'Umar, 'Uthman, Abu Hanifa, al-Shafi'i, al-Tustari, al-Qurashi al-Zuhri, and others such as al-Nawawi. Ibn Hibban devoted a chapter of his *Sahih* to the subject in which he said, commenting the hadith of the Prophet ﷺ: "Whoever fasts all his life has neither fasted nor broken his fast"⁴:

> He means: whoever fasts all his life including the days in which one was forbidden to fast, such as the days of *tashriq*⁵ and the two *'Id*s. By the words: 'he has neither fasted nor broken his fast' he means that he did not in fact fast all his life in order to reap reward for it. For he did not omit [the fasting of] the days in which he was forbidden to fast. That is why the Prophet ﷺ said: 'Whoever fasts all his life, the Fire shall straiten him for this much,' and he counted ninety on his fingers,⁶ meaning the days of his life in which he was forbidden to fast. It does not apply to the person who fasts all his life – being strong enough to do so – without the prohibited days.⁷

Imam al-Nawawi said on the topic:

> Ibn 'Umar fasted permanently, i.e. except the days of 'Id and *tashriq*. This perpetual fast is his way and the way of his father

---

³Quoted in Ibn al-Subki, *Tabaqat al-Shafi'iyya al-Kubra* (4:10).
⁴Narrated from 'Abd Allah ibn 'Amr by Bukhari and Muslim, and from 'Abd Allah ibn al-Shikhkhir by Ahmad, al-Nasa'i, al-Hakim, Ibn Hibban, Ibn Abi Shayba, and others.
⁵The Days of drying the meat after the sacrifice of *'Id al-Adha* = 11, 12, and 13 of Dhu al-Hijja.
⁶Narrated from Abu Musa al-Ash'ari with a sound chain by Ahmad and Ibn Hibban.
⁷As quoted by Ibn Hibban in his *Sahih* (8:349-350). See also Ibn Hajar's notes on the topic in *Fath al-Bari* (1989 ed. 4:222).

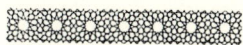 

'Umar ibn al-Khattab, 'A'isha, Abu Talha and others of the *Salaf* as well as al-Shafi'i and other scholars. Their position is that perpetual fasting is not disliked *(makruh)*.[8]

Ibn Qudama states something similar in *al-Mughni* and adds that the same view is related from Ahmad and Malik, and that after the Prophet's ﷺ death Abu Talha fasted permanently for forty years, among other Companions.[9] Ibn Hajar al-Haytami in *al-Khayrat al-Hisan* similarly relates that Abu Hanifa was never seen eating except at night.[10]

The works of al-Bayhaqi count among the treasures of Islamic knowledge for their meticulousness, reliability, and near-perfection in the estimation of the scholars. Among those which have been published are the following:

- *al-Sunan al-Kubra* ("The Major Book of the Prophet's ﷺ *Sunna*s") in about ten large volumes, concerning which Ibn al-Subki said: "No such book was ever compiled in the science of hadith with respect to classification, arrangement, and elegance."

- *Ma'rifa al-Sunan wa al-Athar* ("The Knowledge of *Sunna*s and Reports") in about twenty volumes, which lists the textual evidence of the Shafi'i school under *fiqh* sub-headings. Ibn al-Subki said: "No Shafi'i jurist can do without it," while his father said: "He meant by the title: Al-Shafi'i's Knowledge of the *Sunna*s and Reports."

- *Bayan Khata' Man Akhta'a 'Ala al-Shafi'i* ("The Exposition of the Error of Those Who Attributed Error To al-Shafi'i"). This book complements the *Sunan* and the *Ma'rifa* in the presentation of the textual evidence of the Shafi'i school.

- *al-Mabsut* ("The Expanded [Reference-Book]"), on Shafi'i Law.

---

[8] *Sharh Sahih Muslim*, Kitab 37, Bab 2, #10.
[9] Ibn Qudama, *al-Mughni* (Beirut, 1994 ed. 3:119). For 'Uthman ibn 'Affan, see *Hilya al-Awliya* (1:94 #161).
[10] Al-Haytami, *al-Khayrat al-Hisan* (p. 40).

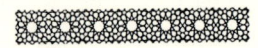

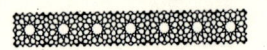

- *al-Asma' wa al-Sifat* ("The Divine Names and Attributes"), concerning which Ibn al-Subki said: "I do not know anything that compares to it."

- *al-I'tiqad 'ala Madhhab al-Salaf Ahl al-Sunna wa al-Jama'a* ("Islamic Doctrine According to the School of the Predecessors Which is the School of the People of the Prophet's ﷺ Way and Congregation of His Companions ؓ") in about forty brief chapters.

- *Dala'il al-Nubuwwa* ("The Signs of Prophethood") in about seven volumes, the foremost large book exclusively devoted to the person of the Prophet ﷺ, as al-Qadi 'Iyad's *al-Shifa' fi Ma'rifa Huquq al-Mustafa* ("The Healing Concerning Knowledge of the Elect Prophet's Rights") is the foremost condensed book on this noble subject.

- *Shu'ab al-Iman* ("The Branches of Belief") in about forteen volumes, in which al-Bayhaqi provides an exhaustive textual commentary on the hadith of the Prophet ﷺ whereby "Belief has seventy-odd branches."[11]

- *al-Da'awat al-Kabir* ("The Major Book of Supplications") in two volumes, which arranges the narrations related to the subject by circumstance, like al-Nawawi's *al-Adhkar* and al-Jazari's similar book.

- *al-Zuhd al-Kabir* ("The Major Book of Asceticism"), which arranges the relevant narrations of the Companions and early Sufis by subject-heading.

- *al-Arba'un al-Sughra* ("The Minor Collection of Forty Hadiths"), which is devoted to the purification of the self and the acquisition of high manners.

- *al-Khilafiyyat* ("The Divergences" [between al-Shafi'i and Abu Hanifa]) of which Ibn al-Subki said: "No-one preceded him in writing a book of this kind, nor followed him in writing its like. It

---

[11]Narrated from Abu Hurayra by Muslim, Ahmad, and others.

is an independent method in hadith science which is appreciated only by experts in both *fiqh* and hadith. It is precious for the texts it contains."

- *Fada'il al-Awqat* ("Times of Particular Merit" [for worship]).

- *Manaqib al-Shafi'i* ("The Immense Merits of al-Shafi'i") in two volumes, which al-Nawawi said was the most reliable book of merits on the Imam. Ibn al-Subki said: "Of *al-I'tiqad, Dala'il al-Nubuwwa, Shu'ab al-Iman, Manaqib al-Shafi'i,* and *al-Da'awat al-Kabir*, I swear that none of them has any peer."

- *Manaqib al-Imam Ahmad* ("The Immense Merits of Imam Ahmad").

- *Tarikh Hukama' al-Islam* ("History of the Rulers of Islam"). Etc.

Ibn al-Subki relates that al-Bayhaqi considered the Prophet's ﷺ references to Abu Musa al-Ash'ari's people to include Abu al-Hasan al-Ash'ari and his school. Al-Bayhaqi said:

> The Prophet ﷺ pointed to Abu Musa al-Ash'ari in relation to the verse: ⟨**Allah will bring a people whom He loves and who love Him**⟩ (5:54) saying: "They are that man's people," due to the tremendous merit and noble rank attributed by this hadith to the imam Abu al-Hasan al-Ash'ari. For he is part of Abu Musa's people and one of his children who have received knowledge and were granted discernment, and he was singled out for strengthening the Sunna and repressing innovation by producing clear proofs and dispelling doubts. It is most likely that the Prophet ﷺ named Abu Musa's people a people beloved by Allah because he knew the soundness of their religion and the strength of their belief. Therefore, whoever leans towards them in the science of the foundations of Religion and follows their position in disowning *tashbih* while adhering to the Book and the Sunna, is one of their number.[12]

Al-Bayhaqi is the last of those who comprehensively compiled the textual evidence of the Shafi'i school including the hadith, the positions of

---

[12] Quoted in Ibn al-Subki, *Tabaqat al-Shafi'iyya al-Kubra* (3:363).

the Imam, and those of his immediate companions. Imam al-Haramayn said: "There is no Shafi'i except he owes a huge debt to al-Shafi'i, except al-Bayhaqi, to whom al-Shafi'i owes a huge debt for his works which imposed al-Shafi'i's school and his sayings."¹³ Al-Dhahabi comments: "Abu al-Ma'ali is right! It is as he said, and if al-Bayhaqi had wanted to found a school of Law for himself he would have been able to do so, due to the vastness of his sciences and his thorough knowledge of juridical differences." Among al-Shafi'i's legal positions reported by al-Bayhaqi is the following in his book *Fada'il al-Awqat*:

> The hadith whereby the Prophet ﷺ forbade the fasting of all of the month of Rajab is weak. Even if it were authentic, its meaning would be that of dislike only, as al-Shafi'i said in the Old School: "I dislike that someone single out the month of Rajab among all other months in order to fast it completely in the way that he completes Ramadan." He also said: "Likewise, that someone single out a specific day among all other days." He continued: "I only disliked it so that an ignorant person will not emulate the one who fasts, thinking that it is obligatory. Otherwise, to fast it is fine *(wa in fa'ala fa hasan)*." Thus al-Shafi'i gave the reason for the reprehensibility [of fasting Rajab] then he said: "But if one fasts it, then fine and good." This is because part of what is universally known among Muslims is that the foundation of the Law said no fast is obligatory except that of Ramadan, whereby the cause for reprehensibilty is lifted.¹⁴

Ibn al-Subki comments:

> On the whole, this text of al-Shafi'i cited by al-Bayhaqi provides a clear proof that to fast the month of Rajab in its entirety is fine and good, and that if the prohibition of fasting it entirely is inauthentic, then the fast remains desirable in the Law. This supports what Shaykh al-Islam al-'Izz ibn 'Abd al-Salam said: "Whoever forbids the fast of Rajab, he is ignorant of the sources of legal rulings." He then expanded on the topic... Nor should any proof against al-Bayhaqi be adduced from the hadith of Ibn 'Abbas prohibiting the

---

¹³Quoted in *Tabaqat al-Shafi'iyya al-Kubra* (4:10-11) and *Siyar A'lam al-Nubala'* (13:532).
¹⁴Quoted in Ibn al-Subki, *Tabaqat al-Shafi'iyya al-Kubra* (4:12).

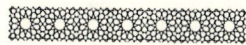 Al-Bayhaqi and the Ash'ari School

fast of Rajab in Ibn Majah's *Sunan* as it has been definitely established to be unsound.[15]

Al-Dhahabi narrates the following relation through al-Bayhaqi: Malik ibn Dinar said: "They say that Malik is an ascetic *(zâhid)*. What asceticism does Malik have when he owns a cloak and other clothes? The only ascetic is 'Umar ibn 'Abd al-'Aziz. The entire world came to him with gaping mouth, but he looked away from it."

Al-Bayhaqi died in Naysabur, at the age of seventy-four.

Imam Abu Al-Hasan Al-Ash'ari

'Ali ibn Isma'il ibn Abi Bishr Ishaq ibn Salim Abu al-Hasan al-Ash'ari al-Yamani al-Basri al-Baghdadi (270-324/330?) was a descendent of the Yemeni Companion Abu Musa al-Ash'ari. In the first half of his scholarly career he was a disciple of the Mu'tazili teacher al-Jubba'i, whose doctrines he abandoned in his fortieth year, at which time he adopted those of *Ahl al-Sunna*. He devoted the next twenty years to the refutation of the *Mu'tazila* and various other sects. Among his books up to the year 320 as listed by himself in *al-'Umad* ("The Supports"):

- *Adab al-Jadal* ("The Etiquette of Disputation").

- *Al-Asma' wa al-Ahkam* ("The Names and the Rulings"), which describes the divergences in the terminology of the scholars and their understanding of the general and the particular.

- *Al-Dafi' li al-Muhadhdhab* ("The Repelling of 'The Emendation'"), a refutation of al-Khalidi's book by that title.

- *Al-Funun* ("The Disciplines"), a refutation of atheists. A second book bearing that title was also written, on the disciplines of *kalâm*.

---

[15] Narrated from Ibn 'Abbas by Ibn Majah with a chain containing Dawud ibn 'Ata', whose weakness is agreed upon as stated in the collective *Sharh Sunan Ibn Majah*.

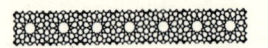

- *Al-Fusul* ("The Sub-Headings") in twelve volumes, a refutation of the philosophers, perennialists, and members of various religions such as Brahmans, Jews, Christians, and Zoroastrians. It contains a refutation of Ibn al-Rawandi's claim that the world exists without beginning.

- *Idah al-Burhan fi al-Radd 'ala Ahl al-Zaygh wa al-Tughyan* ("The Clarification of the Proof in the Refutation of Heretics"), a preliminary to *al-Mujaz*.

- *Al-Idrak* ("The Awareness"), on the disciplines that address the subtleties of dialectic theology.

- *Al-Istita'a* ("Capacity"), a refutation of the *Mu'tazila*.

- *Al-Jawabat fi al-Sifat 'an Masa'il Ahl al-Zaygh wa al-Shubuhat* ("The Replies Pertaining to the Attributes On the Questions and Sophistries of Heretics"), al-Ash'ari's largest work, a refutation of all the Mu'tazili doctrines he had upheld previously.

- *Al-Jawhar fi al-Radd 'ala Ahl al-Zaygh wa al-Munkar* ("The Essence: Refutation of the People of Heresy and Transgression").

- *Al-Jism* ("The Body"), a proof of the *Mu'tazila*'s inability to answer essential questions that pertain to corporeality, contrary to *Ahl al-Sunna*.

- *Jumal al-Maqalat* ("The Sum of Sayings"), which lists the positions of atheists and the positions of monotheists.

- *Khalq al-A'mal* ("The Creation of Deeds"), a refutation of the doctrine of the *Mu'tazila* and *Qadariyya* whereby man creates his own deeds.

- *Al-Luma' fi al-Radd 'ala Ahl al-Zaygh wa al-Bida'* ("The Sparks: A Refutation of Heretics and Innovators"), a slim volume.

- *Al-Luma' al-Kabir* ("The Major Book of Sparks"), a preliminary to *Idah al-Burhan*.

 *Al-Bayhaqi and the Ash'ari School*

- *Al-Luma' al-Saghir* ("The Minor Book of Sparks"), a preliminary to *al-Luma' al-Kabir*.

- *Maqalat al-Falasifa* ("The Sayings of Philosophers").

- *Maqalat al-Islamiyyin* ("Sayings of Those Who Profess Islam"), an encyclopedia of Islamic sects.

- *Al-Masa'il 'ala Ahl al-Tathniya* ("The Questions in Refutation of the Dualists").

- *al-Mujaz* ("The Concise") in twelve volumes, which identifies and describes the various Islamic sects. It contains a refutation of the Shi'i doctrines of the questioning of Abu Bakr al-Siddiq's ﷺ imamate and of the infallibility of the Imam in every era.

- *Al-Mukhtasar fi al-Tawhid wa al-Qadar* ("The Abridgment: On the Doctrine of Oneness and Foreordained Destiny"), a review of the different doctrinal issues which the opponents of *Ahl al-Sunna* are unable to address.

- *Al-Mukhtazan* ("The Safekeeping"), on the questions which opponents did not bring up but which pertain to their doctrines.

- *Al-Muntakhal* ("The Sifted"), a response to questions from the scholars of Basra.

- *Naqd al-Balkhi fi Usul al-Mu'tazila* ("Critique of al-Balkhi and the Principles of the *Mu'tazila*"), a refutation of the book of the Mu'tazili scholar al-Balkhi entitled *Naqd Ta'wil al-Adilla* ("Critique of the Interpretation of the Textual Proofs").

- *Al-Nawadir fi Daqa'iq al-Kalam* ("The Rarities Concerning the Minutiae of Dialectic Theology").

- *Al-Qami' li Kitab al-Khalidi fi al-Irada* ("The Subduer: A Refutation of al-Khalidi's Book on the Will"), a refutation of a-Khalidi's doctrine whereby Allah creates His own will.

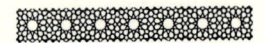

- *Al-Radd ʿala Ibn al-Rawandi* ("Refutation of Ibn al-Rawandi") concerning the Attributes and the Qurʾan.

- *Al-Radd ʿala Muhammad ibn ʿAbd al-Wahhab al-Jubbaʾi*, an extensive refutation of a Muʿtazili scholar and of his book *al-Usul* ("The Principles").

- *Al-Radd ʿala al-Mujassima* ("Refutation of the Anthropomorphists").

- A refutation of ʿAbbad ibn Sulayman in the minutiae of *kalâm*.

- A refutation of a book by ʿAli ibn ʿIsa.

- A refutation of al-Balkhi's book in which the latter claimed he had rectified Ibn al-Rawandi's error in his disputation.

- A refutation of al-Iskafi's book entitled *al-Latif* ("The Subtle").

- A refutation of al-Jubbaʾi on the principles and conditions of scholarly investigation and the derivation of rulings.

- A Refutation of al-Jubbaʾi's objections to al-Ashʿari of the vision of Allah in the hereafter as reported by Muhammad ibn ʿUmar al-Saymari.

- A refutation of al-Khalidi's book on the denial of the vision of Allah in the hereafter.

- A refutation of al-Khalidi's book on the denial of Allah's creation of the deeds of human beings according to His decision.

- The refutation of the philosophers, especially the Perennialist Ibn Qays al-Dahri and Aristotle's books "On the Heavens" and "On the World."

- *Al-Ru'ya* ("The Vision"), which affirms the vision of Allah by the believers in the hereafter, contrary to the Mu'tazili doctrine which denies the possibility of such a vision.

- *Al-Sharh wa al-Tafsil fi al-Radd 'ala Ahl al-Ifk wa al-Tadlil* ("The Detailed Explanation in Refutation of the People of Perdition"), a manual for beginners and students to read before *al-Luma'*.

- *Al-Sifat* ("The Attributes"), a description of the doctrines of the *Mu'tazila, Jahmiyya,* and other sects that differ from *Ahl al-Sunna* on the topic of the divine attributes. It contains a refutation of Abu al-Hudhayl, Ma'mar, al-Nazzam, al-Futi, and al-Nashi, and an affirmation that the Creator possesses a face and hands.

- *Tafsir al-Qur'an wa al-Radd 'ala man Khalafa al-Bayan min Ahl al-Ifki wa al-Buhtan* ("A Commentary on the Qur'an and Refutation of Those Who Contradicted it Among the People of Perdition and Calumny"), in refutation of al-Jubba'i and al-Balkhi.

- Various epistles in response to questions from the scholars of Tabaristan, Khurasan, Arrujan, Sayraf, Amman, Jurjan, Damascus, Wasit, Ramahramuz, Baghdad, Egypt, and Persia.

- *Ziyadat al-Nawadir* ("Addenda to 'The Rarities'").

Among al-Ash'ari's books between the year 320 and his death in 324 as listed by Ibn Furak:

- *Af'al al-Nabi Sallallahu 'Alayhi wa Sallam* ("The Acts of the Prophet ").

- *Al-Akhbar* ("The Reports").

- *Bayan Madhhab al-Nasara* ("Exposition of the Doctrine of Christians").

- *Hikayat Madhahib al-Mujassima* ("The Tales of the Schools of the Anthropomorphists"), a refutation of the proofs they adduce.

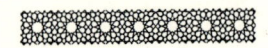

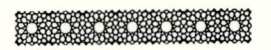

- *Al-Ihtijaj* ("The Adducing of the Proofs").

- *Al-Imama* ("The Doctrine of the Imam").

- *Ithbat al-Qiyas* ("The Upholding of the Principle of Analogy").

- Sessions around the lone-narrator report *(al-khabar al-wâhid)*.

- *Mutashabih al-Qur'an* ("The Ambiguities in the Qur'an"), in which he brought together the stands of the *Mu'tazila* and the atheists in their invalidations of the ambiguities in the hadith.

- *Naqd Ibn al-Rawandi 'ala Ibtal al-Tawatur* ("The Critique of Ibn al-Rawandi's Denial of Mass-Narrated Hadiths"), which contains an affirmation of the principle of Consensus *(ijmâ')*.

- *Naqd al-Mudahat* ("Critique of 'The Similarity'"), a refutation of al-Iskafi on the term *qadar*.

- *Naqd al-Taj 'ala al-Rawandi* ("The Diadem: Critique of Ibn al-Rawandi").

- On questions put to al-Jubba'i concerning names and rulings.

- A refutation of Abu al-Hudhayl on the limitlessness of Allah's foreknowledge and decisions and another on motions.

- A refutation of Harith al-Warraq on the Attributes.

- A refutation of the logicians.

- A refutation of the proponents of metempsychosis and reincarnation.

- *al-'Umad* ("The Supports") on the vision of Allah in the hereafter.

- *Al-Wuquf wa al-'Umum* ("The Abeyance of Rights and the Public at Large").

After listing the above titles, Ibn 'Asakir says: "I have seen other works not mentioned by Ibn Furak in his list." He then proceeds to list the following:

- *Al-Haththth 'ala al-Bahth* ("The Encouragement to Research").

- An epistle on Belief which discusses whether it is permissible to say that belief is created.

- *Risala ila Ahl al-Thughar* ("Epistle to the People of al-Thughar"), a definition on the doctrines of *Ahl al-Sunna*.

Ibn 'Asakir then mentions that al-Ash'ari's works number over two or three hundred books.[16]

The Prophetic Narrations In Praise Of The Ash'aris

The Prophet ﷺ praised the Ash'aris in numerous narrations concerning which al-Qushayri said that they bore not only the external meaning of the tribe of the Companion Abu Musa al-Ash'ari, but also the additional meaning of the followers of his descendent Abu al-Hasan al-Ash'ari, meaning the Ash'ari school. Among these narrations:

- ⟨O you who believe! Whoever among you turns back from his Religion, know that in his stead Allah will bring a people whom He loves and who love Him, humble toward believers, stern toward disbelievers, striving in the way of Allah, and fearing not the blame of any blamer. Such is the grace of Allah which He gives to whom He will. Allah is All-Embracing, All-Knowing.⟩ (5:54) When Allah revealed this verse, the Prophet ﷺ pointed to Abu Musa al-Ash'ari and said: "They are that man's People."[17] Imam Abu al-Qasim al-Qushayri said: "Therefore, the followers of Abu al-Hasan al-Ash'ari are also among his [Abu Musa's] People. For in every place that a people are affiliated to a

---

[16]*Tabyin Kadhib al-Muftari* (p. 129-137).
[17]Narrated from 'Iyad by Ibn Abi Shayba and al-Hakim who said it is *sahih* by Muslim's criterion, and by al-Tabarani with a sound chain as stated by al-Haythami.

Prophet, what is meant is the followers of that Prophet."[18] This is also the position of Ibn 'Asakir, al-Bayhaqi, Ibn al-Subki, and others of the Ash'ari school.[19]

- "Tomorrow shall come to you a people more sensitive in their hearts towards Islam than you." Then the Ash'aris came, among them Abu Musa al-Ash'ari. As they approached Madina they sang poetry, saying: "Tomorrow we meet our beloved ones, Muhammad and his group!" When they arrived they began to shake hands with the people, and they were the first to innovate hand-shaking."[20]

- "The people of Yemen have come to you, most sensitive in their souls, softest of hearts! Belief is from Yemen, wisdom is from Yemen! Pride and arrogance are found among the camel-owners; tranquility and dignity among the sheep-owners."[21]

- "I went in to see the Prophet ﷺ after tying my camel at the gate. People from the Banu Tamim came in to see him. He said: 'Accept the glad tidings, O Banu Tamim!' They said: 'You gave us glad tidings; now give us something tangible.' This exchange took place twice. Then some from the people of Yemen came in to see him. He said: 'Accept the glad tidings, O people of Yemen! for the Banu Tamim did not accept them.' They said: 'We accept, O Messenger of Allah!' Then they said: 'We came to ask you of this Great Matter.' He said: 'Allah was when nothing was other than Him. His Throne stood over the water. He inscribed all things in the Remembrance. He created the heavens and the earth.' Then someone called out: 'You camel has fled, O Ibn al-Husayn!' I darted out and between me and my camel I could see a mirage. By Allah! How I wish that I had left it alone."[22] Ibn al-Subki said: "Our scholars have said that the Prophet ﷺ did not speak to

---

[18] As quoted in al-Qurtubi's *Tafsir* (verse 5:54).
[19] As cited in *Tabyin Kadhib al-Muftari* and *Tabaqat al-Shafi'iyya al-Kubra* (3:362-363).
[20] Hadith of the Prophet ﷺ narrated from Anas ibn Malik with a sound *(sahih)* chain by Ahmad in his *Musnad*.
[21] Hadith of the Prophet ﷺ narrated from Abu Hurayra by Bukhari and Muslim in their *Sahih*s.
[22] Hadith of the Prophet ﷺ narrated from 'Imran ibn Husayn by Bukhari in his *Sahih*.

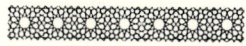 

anyone of the foundations of the Religion *(usûl al-dîn)* in such a way as he has spoken to the Ash'aris in this hadith."[23]

- "They [the Ash'aris] are part of me and I am part of them."[24]

- "The Ash'aris among people are like a precious parcel containing musk."[25]

The Ash'ari School From The Time Of Al-Ash'ari

Ibn 'Abd al-Salam said: "Agreement has formed in subscribing to al-Ash'ari's doctrine among the Shafi'is, the Malikis, the Hanafis, and the nobility of the Hanbalis." His statement was endorsed in his time by the Maliki authority Abu 'Amr ibn al-Hajib and by the Shaykh of the Hanafis Jamal al-Din al-Hasiri.[26] The Maliki imam Abu 'Abd Allah Muhammad ibn Musa al-Mayurqi said: "The *Ahl al-Sunna* among the Malikis, the Shafi'is, and the majority of the Hanafis speak with the tongue of Abu al-Hasan al-Ash'ari and argue by his arguments." Ibn al-Subki quoted it and went on to say: "We do not know any Malikis except they are Ash'aris."[27]

There are some rare exceptions, such as Ibn 'Abd al-Barr and Abu 'Umar al-Talamnaki. As for Ibn Abi Zayd al-Qayrawani (310-386), he belonged to the Ash'ari school which he took, among others, from Abu Bakr ibn 'Abd al-Mu'min the student of Ibn Mujahid the student of Abu al-Hasan al-Ash'ari.[28] Al-Qadi 'Iyad mentioned that in the year 368 Ibn Abi Zayd sent two of his students to deliver some of his books by hand to Ibn Mujahid who

---

[23] Ibn al-Subki, *Tabaqat al-Shafi'iyya al-Kubra* (3:364).
[24] Hadith of the Prophet ﷺ narrated from Abu Musa al-Ash'ari by Bukhari and Muslim.
[25] Hadith of the Prophet ﷺ narrated from Hasan al-Basri in the mode of *mursal* (missing the Companion link) by Ibn Shihab al-Zuhri in Ibn Sa'd's *Tabaqat*. Among those who explained the Ash'aris mentioned in the hadith to include reference to latter-day Ash'aris are Imam Abu al-Qasim al-Qushayri, Ibn al-Subki, and Ibn 'Asakir.
[26] Ibn al-Subki, *Tabaqat al-Shafi'iyya al-Kubra* (3:365).
[27] Ibn al-Subki, *Tabaqat al-Shafi'iyya al-Kubra* (3:366-367).
[28] Al-Darqash, *Abu Muhammad 'Abd Allah ibn Abi Zayd* (p. 109, 237). On Ibn 'Abd al-Barr see Appendix 7, "The Hadith of Allah's 'Descent'" (p. 101).

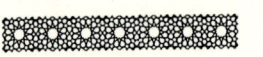

had requested them, with a full licence to narrate them from him *(ijâza)*.[29] Ibn Abi Zayd notably defended the Ash'ari school in his epistle entitled *al-Radd 'ala al-Qadariyya wa Munaqada Risala al-Baghdadi al-Mu'tazili*, a refutation of the attacks of the Mu'tazili 'Ali ibn Isma'il al-Baghdadi.[30] Al-Mayurqi further narrated that Ibn Abi Zayd said: "Al-Ash'ari is a man famous for refuting the people of innovation, the *Qadariyya* and the *Jahmiyya*, and he held fast to the *Sunan*."[31]

Ibn 'Asakir in *Tabyin Kadhib al-Muftari Fi Ma Nasaba ila al-Imam Abi al-Hasan al-Ash'ari* ("The Exposition of the Fabricator's Lies In What He Attributed to al-Ash'ari") and Taj al-Din Ibn al-Subki in *Tabaqat al-Shafi'iyya* listed the most illustrious figures of the Ash'ari scholars, starting with the biographical layer of al-Ash'ari himself.

Al-Ash'ari's Refutation of the *Hashwiyya* and *Mu'tazila*

The Ash'ari scholars were foremost among those who refuted the *Hashwiyya* from the time al-Ash'ari first appeared until that of al-Bayhaqi and Ibn 'Abd al-Salam. Hence al-Bayhaqi in his letter to 'Amid al-Mulk defined the Ash'aris as "Those of the Hanafis, Malikis, and Shafi'is that do not go the way of divesting Allah of His Attributes *(ta'tîl)* as the *Mu'tazila* do, nor the way of likening Allah to creation *(tashbîh)* as the *Mujassima* do."[32] The Ash'aris embodied the Saved Group which holds a middle ground between the vagaries of different heretical doctrines, as described by Ibn 'Asakir:

> The *Hashwiyya*, who liken Allah to creation, said: Allah can be subject to modality and dimension like anything that can be seen. The *Mu'tazila*, the *Jahmiyya*, and the *Najjariyya*[33] said: Allah cannot be seen under any circumstances whatsoever. Al-Ash'ari took the middle

---

[29] Al-Qadi 'Iyad, *Tartib al-Madarik* (4:477). See al-Darqash, *Abu Muhammad 'Abd Allah ibn Abi Zayd* (p. 240-241).
[30] Al-Qadi 'Iyad, *Tartib al-Madarik* (2/4:486-494). See al-Darqash, *Abu Muhammad 'Abd Allah ibn Abi Zayd* (p. 286-287).
[31] Ibn al-Subki, *Tabaqat al-Shafi'iyya al-Kubra* (3:368).
[32] Narrated with its chain by Ibn 'Asakir in *Tabyin Kadhib al-Muftari* (p. 106) and Ibn al-Subki in his *Tabaqat al-Shafi'iyya* (3:396).
[33] The *Najjariyya* were the followers of al-Husayn ibn Muhammad al-Najjar, a third-century Mu'tazili.

road and said: He can be seen without indwelling *(min ghayri hulûl)* and without acquiring limits nor being subject to modality.

The *Najjariyya* said: Allah is in every place without indwelling nor direction. The *Hashwiyya* and *Mujassima* said Allah is materialized *(hâllun)* over the Throne, the Throne is His place, and He sits on it.³⁴ Al-Ash'ari took the middle road and said: Allah existed before there was place; He then created the Throne and the Foot-Stool, and He was in no need of place. He is, after place was created, exactly as He was before it was created.

The *Mu'tazila* said: He has a "hand" *(yad)* but His "hand" is his power *(qudra)* and favor *(ni'ma)*, while His "face" *(wajh)* is His existence. The *Hashwiyya* said: His hand is a limb *(jâriha)*, and His face has a form *(sûra)*.³⁵ Al-Ash'ari took the middle road and said: His hand is an attribute and His face is an attribute, just like His hearing and His sight.

The *Mu'tazila* said: [Allah's] "Descent" *(nuzûl)* is the descent of any given sign of His, or that of His angels, while *istiwâ'* ³⁶ means mastery *(istîlâ')*. The *Mushabbiha* and *Hashwiyya* said: Descent is the descent of His person *(dhât)* through movement *(haraka)* and displacement *(intiqâl)*, and *istiwâ'* is His sitting on the Throne and

---

³⁴The explanation of *istawâ* as *istaqarra* in the verse ⟨Then He established Himself over the Throne⟩ (32:4) is actually reported from al-Kalbi and Muqatil by al-Baghawi – in his commentary entitled *Ma'alim al-Tanzil* (al-Manar ed. 3:488) – who adds that the philologist Abu 'Ubayda [Ma'mar ibn al-Muthanna al-Taymi (d. ~210)] said "He mounted" *(sa'ida)*. Pickthall followed the latter in his translation of the verse as ⟨Then He mounted the Throne⟩. It is a foundational position of the "Salafis" as stated by Imam Muhammad Abu Zahra: "The 'Salafis' and Ibn Taymiyya assert that settledness takes place over the Throne.... Ibn Taymiyya strenuously asserts that Allah descends, and can be above *(fawq)* and below *(taht)* 'without how'.... and that the school of the *Salaf* is the affirmation of everything that the Qur'an stated concerning aboveness *(fawqiyya)*, belowness *(tahtiyya)*, and establishment over the Throne." Abu Zahra, *al-Madhahib al-Islamiyya* (p. 320-322). In contrast, the *Salaf* denied that *istiqrâr* took place over the Throne: Ibn Rushd in *Sharh al-'Utbiyya* stated that Malik's position is: "The Throne is not Allah's location of settledness *(mawdi' istiqrâr Allâh)*." In *Fath al-Bari* (1959 ed. 7:124 #3592).
³⁵This is the "Salafi" position as stated by 'Abd Allah al-Hashidi in his comments on al-Bayhaqi's *al-Asma' wa al-Sifat*: see below, n. 75.
³⁶See Appendix, *"Istiwâ' is a Divine Act"* (p. 89).

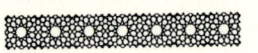

indwelling on top of it.³⁷ Al-Ash'ari took the middle road and said: Descent is one of His attributes and *istiwâ'* is one of His attributes and an action which He did pertaining to the Throne, called *istiwâ'*.³⁸

The *Mu'tazila* said: Allah's speech is created, invented, and brought into being. The *Hashwiyya*, who attribute a body to Allah, said: The alphabetical characters *(al-hurûf al-muqatta'a)*, the materials on which they are written, the colors in which they are written, and all that is between the two covers [of the volumes of Qur'an] is beginningless and preternal *(qadîma azaliyya)*. Al-Ash'ari took a middle road between them and said: The Qur'an is Allah's beginningless speech unchanged, uncreated, not of recent origin in time, nor brought into being. As for the alphabetical characters, the materials, the colors, the voices, the elements that are subject to limitations *(al-mahdûdât)*, and all that is subject to modality *(al-mukayyafât)* in the world – all this is created, brought into being, and invented.³⁹

This is the middle doctrine of *Ahl al-Sunna* which balances between the extremes of complete figurativeness and complete literalism. In his *Maqalat al-Islamiyyin* ("Sayings of Those Who Profess Islam") al-Ash'ari gave another example of this middle doctrine when He rejected the claims of both those who assert that Allah is in every place rather than in a specific place, and those who claim that He is in a specific place rather than in every place:

I. Those who Deny that He is in one place:

[Among] the statements of those who deny that Allah is in a place is the doctrine whereby Allah is materially in every place, and the doctrine whereby He has no end.⁴⁰ Both these sects denied the

---

³⁷Cf. note 34.
³⁸Abu Muhammad al-Tamimi mentioned that two positions were reported from Imam Ahmad concerning *istiwâ'*: One group narrated that he considered it "of the attributes of action" *(min sifât al-fi'l)*, another, "of the attributes of the Essence" *(min sifât al-dhât)*." Ibn Abi Ya'la, *Tabaqat al-Hanabila* (2:296).
³⁹Ibn 'Asakir, *Tabyin Kadhib al-Muftari* (p. 150-151).
⁴⁰Ibn Hibban was expelled from Sijistan for disavowing this doctrine.

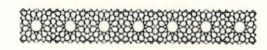

claim whereby Allah is in a specific place at the exclusion of another.

II. Those Who assert that He is in one place:

a) Others said: Allah is a body uncharacterized by any of the attributes of other bodies. He is neither long nor large and cannot be described by color, taste, and touch, nor by any of the attributes of bodies. He is not in things, nor is He on *('alâ)* the Throne except in the sense that He is above it *(fawqah)* without touching it. He is above things and above the Throne, and there is not, between Him and those things, anything other than that He is above them.

b) Hisham ibn al-Hakam said that His Lord was in one specific place exclusively of others, and that that place was the Throne, and that He was in contact with the Throne, and that the Throne contained and circumscribed Him *(hawahu wa haddahu).*

c) One or more of His colleagues said that the Creator fills the Throne and is in contact with it.

d) One or more of those who profess the science of hadith said that the Throne is not entirely filled by Him, for He will make His Prophet sit with Him on the Throne.

III. *Ahl al-Sunna* and the specialists of hadith said that Allah is not a body, nor does He resemble things, and He is on the Throne in the way that He said in the verse: ⟪**The Merciful established Himself over the Throne.**⟫ (20:5) Nor do we venture to speak of its meaning in front of Allah. Rather, we say: *istawa bilâ kayf,* He established Himself without "how."

Ibn Mahdi al-Tabari (d. ~380)

Abu al-Hasan al-Tabari, 'Ali ibn Muhammad ibn Mahdi studied under al-Ash'ari in Basra and Abu al-Hasan al-Bahili, and accompanied Abu Ishaq al-Isfarayini, Abu Bakr ibn Furak, and Abu Bakr ibn al-

Baqillani. His student al-Husayn ibn Aḥmad ibn al-Hasan al-Asadi said: "Our shaykh and teacher Abu al-Hasan al-Tabari was the jurist who authored books in all the sciences. He was erudite, a well of knowledge in jurisprudence, *kalâm*, commentaries of Qur'an, language, and Arabic history. He possessed eloquence and was brilliant at debate. He was peerless in his time." He authored among other works *Al-Usul wa Tafsir Asami al-Rabb* ("Principles of the Religion and the Explanation of the Divine Names") and *Ta'wil Ahadith al-Mushkilat al-Waridat fi al-Sifat* ("The Interpretation of the Problematic Narrations That Pertain to the Attributes"). In the latter book he said: "Allah is 'in the heaven above everything and established over His Throne' in the sense that He is elevated high *('âlin)* above it, and the sense of *istiwâ'* is elevation *(i'tilâ')*."[41] Al-Bayhaqi frequently quotes him in *al-Asma' wa al-Sifat*. He apparently narrated from al-Ash'ari the book *Istihsan al-Khawd fi 'Ilm al-Kalam* ("The Endorsement of the Study of Dialectic Theology") attributed to the latter.[42]

Al-Khattabi (d. 388)

Hamd ibn Muhammad ibn Ibrahim ibn Khattab, Abu Sulayman al-Busti al-Khattabi al-Shafi'i, called by Ibn al-Sam'ani "one of the imams of the Sunna." He was an imam of *fiqh*, a hadith master, a master of the Arabic language, and an erudite scholar. A student of the philologist Abu Sa'id al-A'rabi and the Ash'ari jurisprudent al-Qaffal al-Shashi, he took hadith from Ibn Dasa, Abu al-'Abbas al-Asamm, Abu Bakr al-Najjad, and others. Among those who took hadith from him are al-Hakim, Abu Hamid al-Isfarayini, Ahmad ibn Muhammad al-Harawi – one of those who authored a *Gharib al-Hadith* – Abu Mas'ud al-Karabisi, 'Ali ibn al-Hasan al-Sajzi, al-Fasawi, and others. He authored works in all the sciences, including a commentary on Abu Dawud's *Sunan*; *Kitab al-'Uzla* ("The Book of Seclusion"); *Gharib al-Hadith* ("The Difficult Meanings of Hadith") which al-Dhahabi put on a par with Ibn Sallam and Ibn Qutayba's homonymous works on the subject; *Sharh al-Asma' al-Husna* on which al-Bayhaqi relied a great deal in his *al-Asma' wa al-Sifat*; and *al-Ghunya 'an al-Kalam wa Ahlih* ("The Sufficiency From Dialectic

---

[41] *AS* (p. 410-411); *ASH* (2:308-309).
[42] Ibn al-Subki, *Tabaqat al-Shafi'iyya al-Kubra* (3:466 #230); Ibn 'Asakir, *Tabyin Kadhib al-Muftari* (p. 194).

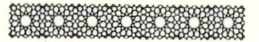

Theology and its Adherents"). In his *Ma'alim al-Sunan* he stated, concerning the narrations of the divine Attributes:

> The people of our time have split into two parties. The first [the *Mu'tazila* and their sub-groups] altogether disavow this kind of hadith and declare them forged outright. This implies their giving the lie to the scholars who have narrated them, that is, the imams of our religion and the transmitters of the Prophetic ways, and the intermediaries between us and Allah's Messenger. The second party [the anthropomorphists] give their assent to the narrations and apply their outward meanings literally in a way bordering anthropomorphism. As for us we steer clear from both views, and accept neither as our school. It is therefore incumbent upon us to seek for these hadiths, when they are cited and established as authentic from the perspectives of transmission and attribution, an interpretation *(ta'wîl)* derived according to the known meanings of the foundations of the Religion and the schools of the scholars, without rejecting the narrations outright, as long as their chains are acceptable and narrators trustworthy.[43]

Al-Halimi (d. 403)

Al-Husayn ibn al-Hasan ibn Muhammad ibn Halim, Abu 'Abd Allah al-Bukhari al-Shafi'i al-Halimi, "the judge, erudite scholar, and foremost leader of the scholars of hadith and *kalâm* in Transoxiana" and one of the hadith masters, he authored important works and is an authority in the Shafi'i school and among early Ash'aris. Al-Hakim took hadith from him and al-Bayhaqi transmitted his scholarship in his *Shu'ab al-Iman* and *al-Asma' wa al-Sifat*.[44]

---

[43] Al-Khattabi, *Ma'alim al-Sunan* (Hims ed. 5:95) in al-Buti, *al-Salafiyya* (p. 140). See also al-Dhahabi, *Siyar A'lam al-Nubala'* 13:3-6 #3626; Ibn al-Subki, *Tabaqat al-Shafi'iyya al-Kubra* 3:282-290 #182.

[44] Al-Dhahabi, *Siyar A'lam al-Nubala'* 13:141-143 #3752, *Tabaqat al-Huffaz* 3:1078.

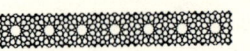

Al-Hâkim (d. 405)

Muhammad ibn 'Abd Allah ibn Muhammad ibn Hamduyah, Abu 'Abd Allah al-Dabbi al-Tamhani al-Naysaburi al-Shafi'i, known as al-Hakim and as Ibn al-Bayyi'. The imam, hadith master, expert in hadith criticism, and shaykh of hadith masters. He took hadith from about two thousand authorities in Khurasan, Iraq, Transoxiana and elsewhere. Among the most prominent of the masters who narrated hadith from him are his own shaykh al-Daraqutni – who declared him stronger in hadith than Ibn Mandah, – al-Bayhaqi, al-Qushayri, and others. Abu Hazim said that al-Hakim was peerless in his time in Khurasan, the Hijaz, al-Sham, Iraq, Rayy, Tabaristan, and Transoxiana. His fame became widespread with lightning speed in his own lifetime. Al-Dhahabi said: "I saw an incredible thing, which is that the *muhaddith* of al-Andalus Abu 'Umar al-Talamnaki copied al-Hakim's book *'Ulum al-Hadith* ("The Sciences of Hadith") in the year 389 from a shaykh which he named, from another narrator, from al-Hakim."

Al-Hakim belongs to the second generation of the Ash'ari school, having taken al-Ash'ari's doctrine at the hands of his students, among them Abu Sahl al-Su'luki. He took *tasawwuf* from Abu 'Amr ibn Nujayd, Abu al-Hasan al-Bushanji, Abu Sa'id Ahmad ibn Ya'qub al-Thaqafi, Abu Nasr al-Saffar, Abu Qasim al-Razi, Ja'far ibn Nusayr, Abu 'Amr al-Zujaji, Ja'far ibn Ibrahim al-Hadhdha', and Abu 'Uthman al-Maghribi.

Al-Hakim said: "I drank water from Zamzam and asked Allah for excellence in writing books." He authored *al-Sahihan* ("The Two Books of *sahîh* Hadiths"), *al-'Ilal* ("The Defects of A Hadith"), *al-Amali* ("The Dictations"), *Fawa'id al-Nusakh* ("Benefits of the Copies"), *Fawa'id al-Khurasaniyyin* ("Benefits of the People of Khurasan"), *Amali al-'Ashiyyat* ("Night Dictations"), *al-Talkhis* ("The Summary"), *al-Abwab* ("The Chapters"), *Tarajim al-Shuyukh* ("Biographies of the Shaykhs"), *Ma'rifa Anwa' 'Ulum al-Hadith* ("Knowledge of the Different Types of the Hadith Sciences"), *Tarikh 'Ulama' Ahl Naysabur* ("History of the Scholars of Naysabur"), *Muzakki al-Akhbar* ("Purified Reports"), *al-Madkhal ila 'Ilm al-Sahih* ("Introduction to the Science of Sound Reports"), *al-Iklil fi Dala'il al-Nubuwwa* ("The Diadem: The Signs of Prophethood"), *al-Mustadrak 'ala al-Sahihayn* ("Supplement for What is Missing From Bukhari and Muslim"), *Ma Tafarrada bi Ikhrajihi Kull Wahidin min al-Imamayn*

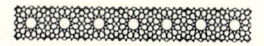

("Reports Found Only in Bukhari or Only in Muslim"), *Fada'il al-Shafi'i* ("The Immense Merits of al-Shafi'i"), *Tarajim al-Musnad 'ala Shart al-Sahihayn* ("The Reports of Ahmad's *Musnad* Which Match the Criteria of the Two Books of *Sahih*"), etc.

It is narrated that a man of letters named Abu al-Fadl al-Hamadhani came to Naysabur where he acquired a following and was named *Badî' al-Zaman* ("Wonder of the Age"), whereupon he became self-infatuated. If he heard someone recite a hundred verses of poetry but once he was able to recite them back from memory, starting from the end and back to the beginning. One day he criticized someone for saying: "So-and-so the memorizer of hadith." He said: "Memorizing hadith! Is it worthy of mention?" When he heard of this, al-Hakim sent him a book of hadith and challenged him to memorize it in a week. Al-Hamadhani returned the book to him and said: "Who can memorize this? 'Muhammad son of So-and-So and Ja'far son of So-and-So reported from So-and-So' — It is filled with all sorts of different names and terms!" Al-Hakim said: "Therefore know yourself, and understand that to memorize such as this is beyond your sphere."

Al-Hakim's *Mustadrak* was criticized by the hadith scholars due to the number of mistakes and inaccuracies found in it. Al-Sakhawi in *al-Tawbikh* and others mention that he declares many forged reports to be rigorously authentic, not to mention weak ones, instead of clinging to his own expressed precondition that only reports with chains of the rank of Bukhari's and Muslim's would be retained. Al-Dhahabi went to excess in regretting that al-Hakim had compiled the *Mustadrak* in the first place.[45] However, the hadith expert Dr. Nur al-Din 'Itr pointed out that al-Hakim compiled it in his old age, intending to revise it, which he did not do beyond the first volume. This is proved by the fact that al-Hakim's mistakes are imperceptible in the first volume of the *Mustadrak*, as confirmed by al-Dhahabi's own minimal corrections.

Another latent criticism is al-Hakim's alleged Shi'ism. Al-Dhahabi in one place names him "one of the oceans of knowledge although a little bit Shi'i" *('alâ tashayyu'in qalîlin fîh)*, in another "al-Hakim the Shi'i," and in another "a famous Shi'i" *(shî'iyyun mashhûr)*. Ibn al-Subki rejects the

---

[45] "It would have been better if al-Hakim had never compiled it"! As mentioned by Dr. Bashshar 'Awwad Ma'ruf published dissertation on al-Dhahabi.

label of Shi'i as baseless since, among other proofs, Ibn 'Asakir in *Tabyin Kadhib al-Muftari* includes al-Hakim among the Ash'aris, who consider the Shi'is innovators. Yet this label is still branded as a blemish today at the hands of those who oppose his positions if they weaken theirs, and those who oppose him for being a follower of al-Ash'ari, or for being a Sufi. As for what al-Dhahabi said about al-Hakim, we must place it in the same category as what he said about the *Mustadrak*.

The first hadith of the Prophet  that al-Hakim narrated in his *Ma'rifa 'Ulum al-Hadith* is: "May Allah make radiant the face of one who heard one of my sayings and then carried it to others. It may be that one carries understanding without being a person of understanding; it may be that one carries understanding to someone who possesses more understanding than he."⁴⁶

On the 3rd of Safar 405 al-Hakim went into the bath, came out after bathing, said "Ah" and died wearing but a waist-cloth before he had time to put on a shirt. Al-Hasan ibn Ash'ath al-Qurashi said: "I saw al-Hakim in my dream riding a horse in a handsome appearance and saying: 'Salvation.' I asked him: 'O al-Hakim! In what?' He replied: 'In writing hadith.'"⁴⁷

Ibn Furak (d. 406)

Muhammad ibn al-Hasan ibn Furak, Abu Bakr al-Asbahani al-Shafi'i, the imam and foremost specialist of *kalâm* and *usûl*, transmitter of al-Ash'ari's school, specialist of Arabic language, grammar, and poetry, orator, jurist, and hadith scholar. He studied doctrine under al-Ash'ari's companion, Abu al-Hasan al-Bahili, and taught al-Qushayri and al-Bayhaqi who cites him frequently in *al-Asma' wa al-Sifat*. He fought and

---

⁴⁶A nearly-mass-narrated *(mashhûr)* sound hadith of the Prophet  reported from several Companions by al-Shafi'i in his *Musnad*, al-Tirmidhi, Abu Dawud, Ibn Majah, Ahmad, al-Darimi, al-Hakim (1:87), al-Tahawi in *Mushkil al-Athar* (2:232), Ibn 'Abd al-Barr in *Jami' Bayan al-'Ilm*, and others. It is also the first hadith al-Ajurri cites in his book *al-Shari'a*.
⁴⁷Ibn 'Asakir, *Tabyin Kadhib al-Muftari* (p. 226-229); al-Dhahabi, *Mizan al-I'tidal* (3:608 #7804, 3:551 #7544) and *Siyar A'lam al-Nubala'* (13:97-106 #3714); Ibn al-Subki, *Tabaqat al-Shafi'iyya al-Kubra* (4:155-171 #329).

defeated the anthropomorphist *Karramiyya* in Rayy then went to Naysabur where he trained generations of *fuqahâ'* at a school founded for him, an expansion of Abu al-Hasan al-Bushanji's earlier Sufi school *(khânkah)*. He brought to Naysabur the transmissions of the narrators of Basra and Baghdad and authored numerous books in various disciplines.

'Abd al-Ghaffar ibn Isma'il said: "Ibn Furak's works in *usûl al-dîn*, *usûl al-fiqh*, and the meanings of the Qur'an count nearly one hundred volumes." Among them: *Mujarrad Maqalat al-Ash'ari* and *Mushkil al-Hadith wa Bayanuh*, in which he refuted both the anthropomorphist tendencies of Hanbali literalists and the over-interpretation of the *Mu'tazila*. Ibn Furak said that he embarked on the study of *kalâm* because of the hadith reported from the Prophet : "The Black Stone is Allah's right hand"[48] which a *mutakallim* explained to his satisfaction in contrast to the *fuqahâ'*.

Ibn Furak was particularly tough on the companions of Imam Ahmad who strayed, in his opinion, from the correct understanding of the verses and hadiths of Allah's attributes. Upon returning from a debate on the topic in Ghazna he fell on the road, poisoned. He was carried back to Naysabur and buried in al-Hira. Ibn 'Asakir relates that his grave is a place of visitation where one seeks healing *(istishfâ')* and one's prayer is answered. Abu 'Ali al-Daqqaq was heard supplicating on behalf of a number of a people and was asked: "Why do you not supplicate on behalf of Ibn Furak?" He replied: "How can I supplicate on his behalf when only yesterday I implored Allah to cure me for the sake of Ibn Furak!"

Ibn Furak said: "The Ash'ari doctrine is that our Prophet – blessings and peace upon him! – is alive in his grave and is Allah's Messenger forever until the end of time, literally, not metaphorically, and that he was

---

[48] Narrated from Ibn 'Abbas, Jabir, Anas, and others by Ibn Abi 'Umar al-Ma'dani in his *Musnad*, al-Tabarani, al-Suyuti in his *Jami' al-saghir* (1:516 #3804-3805), Ibn 'Asakir in *Tarikh Dimashq* (15:90- 92), and others. It is considered *da'if* (weak) by Ibn al-Jawzi, Ibn 'Adi, and Albani, while others consider it forged. Cf. al-Ahdab, *Zawa'id Tarikh Baghdad* (5:321-323 #949). However, al-'Ajluni in *Kashf al-Khafa'* stated that it is *sahîh* as a halted report from Ibn 'Abbas as narrated by al-Quda'i in the wording: "The Corner [of the Black Stone] *(al-rukn)* is Allah's Right Hand on earth...," and declared it *hasan* as a hadith of the Prophet. Its mention in the *Reliance of the Traveller* (p. 853b) as "narrated by al-Hakim, who declared it *sahîh*, from 'Abd Allah ibn 'Amr," is incorrect.

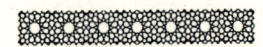

a Prophet when Adam was between water and clay, and his prophethood remains until now, and shall ever remain."⁴⁹

The martyred imam Abu al-Hajjaj Yusuf ibn Dunas al-Findalawi al-Maliki mentioned that Ibn Furak never slept in a house that contained a volume of the Qur'an, but would go and sleep somewhere else out of respect. Among his sayings:

- "Every instance in which you see scholarly endeavor but upon which there is no light: know that it is a secret innovation *(bid'a khafiyya)*." Ibn al-Subki said: "This is truly well-said and shows the great refinement of the teacher. Its foundation is the Prophet's ﷺ saying: 'Uprightness is what the conscience consents to.'"⁵⁰

- "It is impermissible for the *wali* to know that he is a *wali* because it annuls his fear and imposes self-security upon him." Abu 'Ali al-Daqqaq considered it permissible. Al-Qushayri said: "And this is what we prefer, and choose, and declare." Ibn al-Subki said: "Abu al-Qasim is right without the shadow of a doubt, for knowledge of one's *wilaya* does not do away with one's fear of Allah, nor knowledge of one's Prophethood. Indeed, Prophets are the most fearful of Allah of all people, yet they know that they are Prophets. And the *wali* does not cease to fear Allah's planning as long as he lives, and this is the greatest proof of fear. 'Umar said: 'If one of my feet were inside Paradise and the other still outside, I would not feel secure from Allah's plan.'"⁵¹

---

⁴⁹*Tabaqat al-Shafi'iyya al-Kubra* (4:131-132).
⁵⁰Narrated from Abu Tha'laba al-Khushani by Ahmad with a sound chain as stated by al-Haythami in *Majma' al-Zawa'id* (1:175) and Ahmad Shakir in the *Musnad* (13:479 #17671), and from Wabisa ibn Ma'bad al-Asadi by Ahmad and al-Darimi.
⁵¹*Tabyin Kadhib al-Muftari* (p. 230-231); *Siyar A'lam al-Nubala'* (13:130-131 #3739); *Tabaqat al-Shafi'iyya al-Kubra* (4:127-135 #317).

Imam Al-Bayhaqi:
Excerpts From
Allah's Names and Attributes
(AL-ASMA' WA AL-SIFAT)

AS = al-Kawthari ed.
ASH = al-Hashidi ed.

بسم الله الرحمن الرحيم

The Shaykh, the Imam, the hadith master, Abu Bakr Ahmad ibn al-Husayn ibn 'Ali al-Bayhaqi – may Allah Almighty have mercy on him – said: "This is the book of the Names and Attributes of Allah Exalted and Almighty, which are firmly established by Allah's Book, or the Sunna of Allah's Messenger ﷺ or the Consensus of the *Salaf* of this Community before the division befell and innovation appeared.[52]

What Allah Is Not

It is obligatory to hold and believe of the Creator several things, among them, to affirm that He is neither an indivisible substance *(jawhar)* nor an accident *('arad)*, thereby affirming His exemption from likeness to anything created *(tashbîh)*.[53]

The Self-Exalted *(Al-Muta'âl)*

The meaning of "The Self-Exalted" *(al-Muta'âl)* is The Elevated *(al-Murtafi')*, meaning elevated above any of the possibilities that characterize creatures.... [Among them] Displacement from one place to another.[54]

---

[52] AS (p. 3); ASH (1:15-16). See Appendix 1, "Allah's Beautiful Names" (p. 55).
[53] AS (p. 8); ASH (1:35).
[54] AS (p. 34); ASH (1:97).

The Most Hidden *(Al-Bâtin)*

Al-Halimi said: The meaning of "The Most Hidden" *(al-Bâtin)* is He Who is not perceived by the senses, but is perceived through His marks and acts. Al-Khattabi said: The meaning of "appearance" *(al-zuhûr)* and "hiding" *(al-butûn)* may be respectively His manifestation to the insights of those who reflect, and his veiling from the sights of those who look with their eyes. Its meaning may also be the Knower of all manifest matters and the Aware of all hidden and concealed ones.[55]

The All-Hearing *(Al-Samî')*

Al-Halimi said: The meaning of "The All-Hearing" *(al-Samî')* is He Who perceives the sounds which creatures perceive with their ears, but without his having ears.[56]

The All-Seeing *(Al-Basîr)*

The meaning of "The All-Seeing" *(al-Basîr)* is He Who perceives the objects and colors which creatures perceive with their sights, without His having the organ of eye.[57]

The Witness *(Al-Shahîd)*

The meaning of "The Witness" *(al-Shahîd)* is He Who is well aware of all that creatures can know only by way of witnessing while being present. . . because a human being who is far away is subject to the limitation and shortcomings of his sensory organs, while Allah Almighty is not endowed

---

[55] *AS* (p. 35); *ASH* (1:98-99).
[56] *AS* (p. 44); *ASH* (1:120).
[57] *AS* (p. 45); *ASH* 1:122-123.

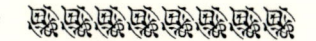

with sensory organs nor subject to the limitations of those who possess them.[58]

Allah's "Nearness" And His "Cover"

About the Prophet's ﷺ hadith: "Allah shall bring the believer near Him until He shall lower His cover upon him and hide him from people."[59] The meaning of "He brings the believer near Him" is that He brings him near His bountiful gifts, and the meaning of "He lowers His cover upon him" is His tenderness, kindness, and care.[60]

The Unity Of *Tawhîd*

About the Prophet's ﷺ hadith: "I was ordered to fight people until they say: 'There is no God but Allah.' When they say it, they have made untouchable by me their life and property, apart from the rights due upon them."[61] Abu 'Abd Allah al-Halimi said: In this hadith there is explicit proof

---

[58] *AS* (p. 46-47); *ASH* (1:126-127).
[59] Narrated from Ibn 'Umar by Bukhari and Muslim. The complete hadith states: A man asked Ibn 'Umar: "What did you hear the Prophet ﷺ say about private conversation [with Allah] on the Day of Resurrection?" Ibn 'Umar said: I heard Allah's Messenger ﷺ say: "Allah shall bring the believer near Him until He shall lower His cover upon him and hide him from people. Then He will say to him: 'Do you know this sin? Do you know that sin?' He will reply: 'Yes, O yes, my Lord!' Then He will say to him again: 'Do you know this sin? Do you know that sin?' Again he will reply: 'Yes, O yes, my Lord!' Until he stands convicted for his sins and considers himself lost. Then Allah will say: 'I covered them up for you in the world, and I am forgiving them for you today.' Then he will be given his record of good deeds. As for the disbelievers and the hypocrites, the witnesses shall say of them: 'Here are the ones who belied their Lord. Allah's curse be on the transgressors!'"
[60] *AS* (p. 56); *ASH* (1:150-151). Ibn al-Jawzi said in *Daf' Shubah al-Tashbih* (1998 Kawthari repr. p. 47): "The scholars said that [it means] Allah brings one near His mercy *(rahma)* and subtle kindness *(lutf)*, while Ibn al-Anbari said that His cover is His custody *(hiyâta)* and shield *(sitr)*."
[61] A mass-narrated *(mutawâtir)* hadith of the Prophet ﷺ narrated by Bukhari, Muslim, and others from nineteen Companions as stated by al-Kattani in *Nazm al-Mutanathir*.

that that declaration *(lâ ilâha illallâh)* suffices to extirpate oneself from all the different kinds of disbelief in Allah Almighty.⁶²

Allah's Speech

The meaning of the Prophet's ﷺ saying: "It came out of Him"⁶³ is that it proceeds from Him *(wujida minh)* whereby He spoke it and revealed it upon his Prophet ﷺ and He made it intelligible to His servants. This "coming out" is not like our speech, for Allah is everlasting and possesses no inside *(lâ jawfa lah)* – greatly exalted is He above any resemblance to creatures! However, Allah's speech is one of His attributes, pre-existent *(azalî)*, existing in His person *(sifatun lahu azaliyya mawjûdatun bi dhâtihi)*. He always was, and continues to be, ever described by it.⁶⁴

The Recitation Of The Qur'an⁶⁵

The Qur'an which we recite is Allah's speech literally recited with our tongues, written in our volumes, preserved in our chests, and heard with our hearing, without indwelling in any of the preceding. It is one of the attributes of Essence and is inseparable from Him. This is exactly the same as the Creator being known in our hearts, mentioned by our tongues, written in our Books, worshipped in our mosques, and heard with our hearing, without indwelling in any of the above. As for our recitation, writing, and

---

⁶²*AS* (p. 96); *ASH* (1:235). This is identical to Malik's saying as reported by al-Shafi'i: "Oneness is exactly what the Prophet ﷺ said: 'I was ordered to fight people until they say There is no God but Allah.' So, whatever makes blood and property untouchable – that is the reality of declaring Allah's Oneness *(haqîqa al-tawhîd)*." Narrated by al-Dhahabi from al-Sulami in *Siyar A'lam al-Nubala'* (8:386). The Ash'ari position as represented by al-Halimi is reiterated by al-Nawawi in his commentary on this hadith in *Sharh Sahih Muslim*. Al-Nawawi added: "The texts show that the Prophet contented himself with [requiring] assent to what he brought, without asking one to know the proof as pre-condition."

⁶³In the hadith: "In truth you do not return to Allah with anything better than what came out of Him, meaning the Qur'an." Narrated from Abu Dharr by al-Tirmidhi and al-Hakim but declared weak by al-Bukhari in *Khalq Af'al al-'Ibad*.

⁶⁴*AS* (p. 236-237); *ASH* (1:576-578, 2:22).

⁶⁵See Appendix 2, "The Controversy Over the Pronunciation of the Qur'an" (p. 59).

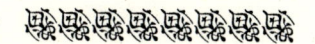

memorization of the Qur'an, they are part of what we earn *(min iktisâbina)* – and what we earn is without doubt created.⁶⁶

Concerning the hadith of the Prophet ﷺ: "If the Qur'an were inside an untanned hide the Fire would not touch it."⁶⁷ Ibrahim ibn Hani' said: I heard Ahmad ibn Hanbal say about 'Uqba ibn 'Amir's narration: "'Inside an untanned hide' means in a man's heart. It is hoped that those who have the Qur'an well-preserved in their heart will not be touched by the Fire."⁶⁸

Ibn al-Mubarak said: "I do not say the Qur'an is the Creator nor that it is created. Rather, it is Allah's speech, inseparable from Him." This is the position of the *Salaf* and *Khalaf* among the major scholars of hadith. Namely, that the Qur'an is Allah's speech and one of the Attributes of His Entity, inseparable from Him. . . .

Two positions are retained from the *Salaf* concerning our recitation, writing, and memorization of the Qur'an. Some have made a distinction between recitation *(tilâwa)* and the thing recited *(matluw)*, as we have; others have preferred not to speak about it, at the same time as they rejected the claim of those who said: "My pronunciation *(lafzî)* of the Qur'an is uncreated."⁶⁹

---

⁶⁶*AS* (p. 258-259); *ASH* (2:5).
⁶⁷Narrated from 'Uqba ibn 'Amir by Ahmad with three chains in his *Musnad*, al-Darimi in his, al-Tahawi in *Mushkil al-Athar* (1:390), al-Tabarani in *al-Kabir* (308 #850), and Abu Ya'la in his *Musnad* (3:284). All of their chains are weak as they are narrated through 'Abd Allah ibn Lahi'a from Mishrah ibn 'Ahan Abu al-Mus'ab al-Ma'afiri. The over-lenient editor of the *Musnad* Hamza al-Zayn declares the hadith fair (13:353 #17298, 363 #17340, 367 #17351), but Imam Ahmad himself in *al-'Ilal wa Ma'rifa al-Rijal* (3:268 #5190) alluded that the chain was defective, as Ibn Lahi'a first used not to trace its text back to the Prophet ﷺ. Hence the editors of Abu Ya'la's *Musnad* (3:284 #1745) and al-Bayhaqi's *al-Asma' wa al-Sifat* (*ASH* 2:14-15 #582), Asad and al-Hashidi, both declare its chains weak. The latter mentions that it is also narrated through a much weaker chain by al-Tabarani (6:172 #5901, 17:186 #498) and others, which does not strengthen the narration. Ibn Qutayba categorically declares the hadith false in *Ta'wil Mukhtalaf al-Hadith* (p. 200) because, he says, "we can see volumes of the Qur'an burn and suffer what other accidents *('urûd)* and books suffer." However, al-Munawi in *Fayd al-Qadir* indicated that it is strengthened by other chains and mentioned that al-Baghawi cited it *Sharh al-Sunna*, which shows that he considered the hadith valid.
⁶⁸Narrated with a sound chain to Imam Ahmad.
⁶⁹*AS* (p. 264-265); *ASH* (2:14-17).

Something Ibn Shaddad had written was handed to Abu Bakr al-Marwazi which containing the phrase: "My pronunciation of the Qur'an is uncreated" and the latter was asked to show it to Ahmad ibn Hanbal for corroboration. The latter crossed out the phrase and wrote instead: "The Qur'an, however used *(haythu yusraf)*, is uncreated."[70]

In another sound narration, Abu Bakr al-Marwazi, Abu Muhammad Fawran [or Fawzan], and Salih ibn Ahmad ibn Hanbal witnessed Ahmad rebuking one of his students named Abu Talib with the words: "Are you telling people that I said: 'My pronunciation of the Qur'an is uncreated'?" Abu Talib replied: "I only said this from my own." Ahmad said: "Do not say this – neither from me, nor from you! I never heard any person of knowledge say it. The Qur'an is Allah's speech uncreated, whichever way it is used." Salih said to Abu Talib: "If you told people what you said, now go and tell the same people that Abu 'Abd Allah [Imam Ahmad] forbade to say it."[71]

Allah's Self *(Nafs)*

One speaks of Allah as a Self *(nafs)* but not in the sense that He possesses an animate soul *(nafs manfûsa)* nor in the sense of a body into which spirit was breathed *(jism murawwah)*. One explanation of His saying: ⟨**You know what is in myself and I know not what is in Yourself**⟩ (5:116) is: You know what I hide within and keep secret, whereas I know not what you make invisible and conceal away from me. An example of this is the

---

[70] *AS* (p. 265); *ASH* (2:18). Narrated with a sound chain by Bayhaqi. Al-Kawthari commented on this and the next narration as follows: "Due to such equivocal expressions, many of Ahmad's companions erroneously thought that anything remotely connected with the Qur'an is preternal *(qadîm)*. Bukhari said in *Khalq Af'al al-'Ibad*: 'As for what the two parties from the school of Ahmad have claimed as proof, each for his own position: Much of what they relate is not established as authentic. It is probable they did not comprehend the subtleness of his position. What is known from Ahmad and the people of knowledge is that Allah's speech is uncreated and all else is created. But they hated to discuss and explore obscure matters, avoiding dialectic theologians and their queries and disputations, except in what was a matter of knowledge and which the Prophet ﷺ had clarified.'"

[71] *AS* (p. 265-266); *ASH* (2:18). This is a sound narration also found in Salih ibn Ahmad's book *al-Mihna* (p. 70-71), Ibn al-Jawzi's *Manaqib al-Imam Ahmad* (p. 155), and Ibn Taymiyya in *Majmu' al-Fatawa* (12:360, 12:425).

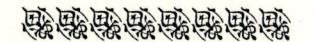

Prophet's ﷺ saying [in the divine hadith]: "If he mentions Me in Himself I mention him in Myself, and if He comes near Me one hand-span I come near him a cubit."[72] That is: No-one knows nor sees this mention. As for the two instances of "coming near," what is meant by them is to express the swiftness of Allah's response and forgiveness, as we narrated that Qatada said.

As for Allah's jealousy mentioned in the hadith of Ibn Mas'ud – "No-one is more jealous *(aghyar)* than Allah"[73]– it means that no-one is able to reprimand more severely *(azjar)* than Allah. For Allah is jealous in the sense that He is severe, reprimands us for disobeying Him, and dislikes vile actions.[74]

Allah's Form *(Sûra)*

It is impermissible that the Creator be attributed form *(sûra)*, nor does He possess form, because form is variegated *(mukhtalifa)* and appearances are mutually contrasted *(al-hay'ât mutadâdda)*. Because of their mutual contrast He cannot be described as having them in general; likewise, he cannot be described as having one of them in particular.[75]

What is obligatory for us and every Muslim to know is that our Lord is not endowed with a form nor a physiognomy *(laysa bi dhî sûra wa lâ hay'a)*. For form requires modality, which is precluded from Allah and from His Attributes.

---

[72] Narrated from Abu Hurayra by Bukhari and Muslim: "I am as My servant thinks of Me, and I am with him when He remembers Me. If he mentions Me in Himself I mention him in Myself. If he mentions Me in a gathering, I mention him in a better gathering. If He comes near Me one span I come near him one cubit. If he comes near Me one cubit I come near him an arm's length. If he comes to Me walking, I come to him running."
[73] Narrated *marfû'* by Bukhari and Muslim.
[74] AS (p. 286); ASH (2:53-54).
[75] AS (p. 289); ASH (2:60). Cf. Ibn al-Jawzi in *Daf' Shibah al-Tashbih* (1998 Kawthari repr. p. 35): "Know that it is obligatory upon every Muslim to firmly hold that it is impermissible to attribute to Allah ﷺ form *(sûra)*, which consists in physiognomy *(hay'a)* and combination *(ta'lîf)*." The "Salafi" editor of *Al-Asma' wa al-Sifat*, 'Abd Allah al-Hashidi, openly attributes form and shape to Allah. He states (2:60): "As for our Lord, we affirm that He possesses a form *(sûra)*" and (2:67) "As for us we affirm a form *(sûra)* for Allah unlike forms." Note that the *Karramiyya* said: "Allah is a body unlike bodies." Dhahabi, *Siyar* (10:10).

About the Prophet's ﷺ hadith: "On the Day of Resurrection, Allah shall come to the people in the form *(sûra)* that is familiar to them."⁷⁶ This can be interpreted to mean that He shall come to them in the attribute *(sifa)* that is familiar to them. . . . What confirms this interpretation is the Prophet's ﷺ saying in the narration of 'Ata' ibn Yasar from Abu Sa'id al-Khudri: "Then Allah will come to them in a form lower [or more suitable] *(adnâ)* than the one wherein they had seen Him,"⁷⁷ whereas they had not seen Him at all prior to this. One understands therefore that the meaning of "form" here is "attribute."⁷⁸

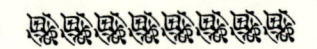

Allah's Hand, Palm, Fingers, etc.

Some of the keenest scholars have said that the Right *(al-yamîn)* signifies the Hand *(al-yad)*, and the Palm *(al-kaff)* likewise, in the sense that the hand for Allah is an attribute, not a limb.⁷⁹ Thus every passage that mentions it in the Book and the authentic Sunna carries a meaning in connection with the object of mention such as folding up, taking, seizing, spreading, sweeping, accepting, giving, and other acts connecting the personal Attributes to what those attributes entail, without touch nor contact. There is never in all this any likeness between Allah and creation whatsoever. Others have said that the handful *(al-qabda)* [in the verse ⦃The whole earth is His handful on the Day of Resurrection⦄ (39:67)] may be by means of a limb – exalted is Allah high above that! – while others said that it may mean dominion *(al-mulk)* and power *(al-qudra)*. . . . as in His saying: ⦃From among those whom your right hands possess⦄ (30:28) which signifies property. It was also said that by the verse ⦃And the heavens are rolled in His right hand⦄ (39:67) is

---

⁷⁶Narrated in a long hadith from Abu Hurayra and Abu Sa'id al-Khudri by Bukhari and Muslim.

⁷⁷Narrated by Bukhari.

⁷⁸*AS* (p. 296); *ASH* (2:70). Abu Sulayman al-Khattabi said: "The meaning of 'Allah shall come to the people etc.' is that He shall lift the veil for them so that they shall see Him with the eyes *(hattâ yarawnahu 'iyânan)* just as they used to know Him in the world through proofs *(kamâ kânû 'arafûhu fî al-dunyâ istidlâlan)*. And the sight of Him after they used not to see Him, is equivalent to the coming of someone never seen heretofore." In Ibn al-Jawzi, *Daf' Shubah al-Tashbih* (1998 al-Kawthari repr. p. 35). See also Appendix 3, "The Vision of Allah in the World and the Hereafter" (p. 71).

⁷⁹Cf. Imam Malik, see Appendix 4, "Allah's 'Hand'" (p. 81).

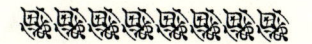

meant that the heavens are bound to disappear according to his oath. That is, He swore an oath to abolish them. . . .

About the Prophet's ﷺ hadith: "No-one spends something good in charity – and Allah accepts nothing but good – except the Merciful takes it with His right hand, if only a date; it increases in the palm of the Merciful until it exceeds the size of a mountain, just as one of you makes his parcel of land productive."[80] His saying "The Merciful's palm" *(kaff)* means His dominion and sovereignty according to the keenest scholars.[81]

About the hadith whereby a Jew – or: one of the rabbis – said to the Prophet ﷺ: "Allah places the heavens on a finger, the earths on a finger, the trees on a finger, the undersoil on a finger, and all creatures on a finger." Hearing this, the Prophet ﷺ smiled until his molar teeth showed. Some versions state: "he smiled in confirmation of the rabbi's words." Then he said: ❰And they esteem not Allah as He has the right to be esteemed❱ (39:67).[82] Abu Sulayman al-Khattabi said:

> The Jews are anthropomorphists, and they claim that part of the revealed Torah consists in expressions that support anthropomorphism. However, the Muslims do not accept such expressions among their doctrines. It is established that the Prophet ﷺ said: "Whatever the People of the Book narrate to you, neither believe nor disbelieve them, but say: **'We believe in Allah and whatever was revealed to us.'** (2:136)"[83] The Prophet ﷺ is the most apt of all creation to have applied this command in the above report. The proof for the veracity of this fact is that he did not utter a single word to confirm nor deny it. All that he let show was a smile, which in one case expresses approval, in another, surprise and disapproval. Then he recited the verse which may apply to either case, but there is no mention of fingers in the verse. As for the words of one of the narrators – "in

---

[80]Narrated from Abu Hurayra by Muslim, Ahmad, al-Nasa'i, Ibn Majah, and al-Tirmidhi who said it is *hasan sahih*.
[81]*AS* (p. 330-331); *ASH* (2:159-160).
[82]Narrated from 'Amr ibn Hafs ibn Ghyath by Bukhari and Muslim.
[83]Narrated from Abu Hurayra by Bukhari. The complete narration states: "The People of the Book would read the Torah in Hebrew and explain it in Hebrew to the People of Islam, whereupon the Prophet ﷺ said: 'Neither believe nor disbelieve the People of the Book, but say: ❰We believe in Allah and whatever was revealed to us.❱ (2:136)

confirmation of the rabbi's words" – they are pure speculation, and the matter of this supposed confirmation remains a weak view fow what he let show does not explicitly disclose one view over the other.... To adduce a proof from smiling or laughter in such a tremendous instance is therefore not allowed in the presence of two conflicting interpretations for the evidence.[84]

About the Prophet's ﷺ hadith: "There is no heart except it lies between the two fingers of the Merciful. If He wishes, He will set it aright; and if He wishes, He will lead it astray."[85] It means that the hearts are under his power and dominion. They were mentioned specifically because Allah Almighty has made the heart the seat of passing thoughts, will, resolutions and intentions, which are all the introductories of actions. Then He made all the limbs dependent on the heart in their motions and stillness, thereby showing that our actions are all measured out by Allah and created, and that nothing happens without His will. The Prophet ﷺ exemplified for His Companions Allah's preternal power with the illustration clearest to their own understandings,[86] for none has more power over something than when he has it between his fingers. It may also mean the two favors of benefit and protection, or the two traces of Allah's favor and justice.[87]

The Method In Interpreting The Attributes

The rule is that every attribute mentioned in the Book, or authentically conveyed in mass-narrated *(mutawâtir)* reports, or in lone-narrated ones *(âhâd)* but having an origin *(asl)* in the Book, or being inferable from one of its meanings: we affirm such an attribute and we let it pass as stated in its external wording, without addressing modality. As for what is not mentioned

---

[84]*AS* (p. 334-338); *ASH* (2:169-170). Al-Qurtubi explained the Prophet's ﷺ smile here to mean disapproval in light of the verse that follows it. Cf. *AS* (p. 336).
[85]Narrated from 'Abd Allah ibn 'Amr by Muslim and from al-Nawwas ibn Sam'an by Ahmad, al-Nasa'i, Ibn Majah, Ibn Hibban in his *Sahih*, al-Hakim, and others, all with sound chains. Al-Hakim declared the hadith sound and al-Dhahabi concurred. The continuation of the hadith states that the Prophet ﷺ used to say: "O Transformer of hearts! Make firm our hearts in Your Religion," and that he also said: "And the balance is in the Merciful's hand, He elevates a people while he abases others, and so until the Day of Resurrection."
[86]This is also al-Wahidi's (d. 468) explanation in his *Asbab al-Nuzul* (p. 312 #774).
[87]*AS* (p. 341); *ASH* (2:174). Also see Appendix 4, "Allah's 'Hand'" (p. 81).

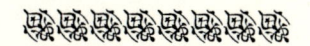

in the Book, nor originates in mass-narrated reports, nor derives from the meanings of the Book, at the same time being conveyed in lone-narrated reports: if, by letting it pass according to its external meaning, we end up likening Allah to creation, then we interpret that meaning on linguistic bases so as to eliminate any anthropomorphism.[88]

The Beginning of Creation

Allah ﷻ said: ⟨He it is Who produces creation then reproduces it⟩ (30:27).

'Abd Allah ibn 'Amr ibn al-'As narrated that the Prophet ﷺ said: "Allah foreordained *(qaddara)* all the destinies *(al-maqâdîr)* before creating the heavens and the earth by fifty thousand years."[89]

'Imran ibn Husayn narrated:

I went in to see the Prophet ﷺ after tying my camel at the gate. People from the Banu Tamim came in to see him. He said: "Accept the glad tidings, O Banu Tamim!" They said: "You gave us glad tidings; now give us something tangible." This exchange took place twice. Then some from the people of Yemen came in to see him. He said: "Accept the glad tidings, O people of Yemen! for the Banu Tamim did not accept them." They said: "We accept, O Messenger of Allah!" Then they said: "We came to ask you of this Great Matter." He said: "Allah was when nothing was other than Him. His Throne stood over the water. He inscribed all things in the Remembrance. He created the heavens and the earth." Then someone called out: "You camel has fled, O Ibn al-Husayn!" I darted out and between me and my camel I could see a mirage. By Allah! How I wish that I had left it alone.[90]

---

[88] *AS* (p. 353); *ASH* (2:194-195).
[89] Narrated from 'Abd Allah ibn 'Amr ibn al-'As by al-Tirmidhi *(hasan sahîh gharîb)* and Ahmad; also by Muslim with the following wording: "Allah inscribed *kataba*) the destinies of all created things before creating the heavens and the earth by fifty thousand years, while His Throne stood over the water *(wa 'arshuhu 'alâ al-mâ')*."
[90] Narrated from 'Imran ibn Husayn by Bukhari in his *Sahih*. Ibn al-Subki said: "Our scholars have said that the Prophet ﷺ did not speak to anyone of the foundations of the Religion *(usûl al-dîn)* in such a way as he has spoken to the Ash'aris [= Yemenis] in this hadith." Ibn al-Subki, *Tabaqat al-Shafi'iyya al-Kubra* (3:364).

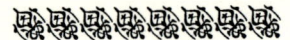

His words "Allah was when nothing was other than Him" indicate that there was nothing else other than Him – neither water, nor the Throne, nor anything else, since all of that is "other than Him." His words: "His Throne stood over the water" means that He then created water, and He created the Throne over the water, after which He inscribed all things in the Remembrance, as we narrated in the hadith of 'Abd Allah ibn 'Amr ibn al-'As. This above is most obvious in the hadith of Abu Razin al-'Uqayli.

The latter narrated that the Prophet ﷺ disliked to be asked [too many] questions, but when [he,] Abu Razin [,] asked him a question it pleased him. He said:

I said: "O Messenger of Allah, where was[91] our Lord before He created the heavens and the earth?" He replied: "He was in a mist *(kâna fî 'amâ')* above which there was air *(mâ fawqahu hawâ')* and below which there was air *(wa mâ tahtahu hawâ')*. Then He created the Throne over the water."[92]

If the original text has *'amâ'* it means a kind of mist or thin cloud *(sahâb raqîq)*. By the words "in a mist" he means "over the cloud, disposing of it at will *(mudabbiran lahu)* and self-exalted over it *('âliyan 'alayh)*," just as He ﷺ said: ⟨Have you taken security from Him Who is in the heaven⟩ (67:16) meaning Him Who is above the heaven, and ⟨I shall crucify you

---

[91] Ibn al-'Arabi in *'Arida al-Ahwadhi* states that the word "where" in Abu Razin's question refers to rank, not place *(al-makâna dûn al-makân)*, as cited by al-Kawthari in *AS* (p. 376 n. 2).
[92] Narrated from Abu Razîn al-'Uqayli (Laqit ibn Sabura) by al-Tirmidhi *(hasan)*, Ibn Majah, Ahmad with two chains, Ibn Hibban in his *Sahih*, al-Tabarani in *al-Kabir* (19:207 #468), and others. Al-Tirmidhi added that Ahmad [ibn Mani'] the narrator of this hadith said: "Yazid [ibn Harun] said: 'The mist means there was nothing with Him.'" All of the above chains, like al-Bayhaqi's, are through Waki' ibn Hudus or 'Uds whose rank as a narrator is unknown according to Yahya ibn al-Qattan and al-Dhahabi but whom Ibn Hajar deemed "acceptable" *(maqbûl)*, i.e. for follow-ups but not for hadiths which he alone reports. Consequently the chain is weak *(da'îf)* as stated by al-Arna'ut in *Sahih Ibn Hibban* (14:8-10 #6141), al-Hashidi in *ASH* (2:235 #801), and al-Albani in Ibn Abi 'Asim's *al-Sunna* (p. 271-272 #612). There is a further problem with Hammad ibn Salama also being the only one who reports this hadith, as discussed by al-Kawthari in his marginalia on *al-Sayf al-Saqil* (p. 109-112). Ibn Qutayba in *Mukhtalaf al-Hadith* (p. 221) also considers this narration inauthentic.

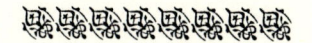

"in" *(fi)* **the trunks of palm-trees⟩** (20:71) meaning on their trunks.[93] His saying "above which there was air" means "there was air above the cloud"; likewise, "below which there was air" means "there was air under the cloud."[94]

It was also said that the actual word is *'imâ* – blind void – which means "nothing determined" *(lâ shay'un thâbit)*, as it is part of what creatures are blind to, because it is other-than-something, just as he said in the hadith of 'Imran ibn Husayn ﷺ. Then he said: "Neither was there air above it, nor below it *(mâ fawqahu wa lâ tahtahu hawâ')*."[95] That is, there was not, above the blind void which is nothing existent, any air, nor was there below it any air. For if this is other-than-something, then it cannot possibly be attributed air in any way whatsoever, and Allah knows best. Abu 'Ubayd [al-Qasim ibn Sallam] al-Harawi, the author of the two *Gharib*s said: "Some of the people of knowledge said that it means 'Where was the Throne of our Lord?' phrased elliptically by way of abridgment, as in His saying: ⟨**And ask the**

---

[93] Al-Mubarakfuri in *Tuhfa al-Ahwadhi* (8:420) cites al-Khazin's quotation of al-Bayhaqi's text followed by that of al-Suyuti in *Misbah al-Zujaja* who says: "The qadi Nasir al-Din ibn al-Munayyar said: 'The problem of this hadith resides in circumstantiality *(al-zarfiyya)*, aboveness *(al-fawqiyya)*, and belowness *(al-tahtiyya)*. The answer is that 'in' *(fi)* means 'over' *('alâ)*, and 'over' means 'establishing dominion' *(istîlâ')*. That is: He was in control over *(mustawlî 'alâ)* this cloud out of which He created all created things.... above and under which there was air. It was also narrated with the wording: *'imâ* in shortened form, which means the non-existence *('adam)* of everything other than Him, as if he were saying: 'He was and nothing existed together with Him, rather, everything was non-existent, a blind void, neither existent nor seen.' The 'air' is also the vacuum of non-existence *(al-farâgh al-'adam)*, as if he were saying: 'He was and there was nothing with Him, no *above*, and no *below*.'"

[94] Al-Kawthari read the passage to mean "above which there was *no* air *(mâ fawqahu hawâ')* and below which there was *no* air *(wa mâ tahtahu hawâ')*," commenting: "This is an explicit proof-text that what is meant by the cloud *(al-sahâb)* is not the known cloud which has air above and below it, but an emblematic cloud *(al-sahâb al-ma'nawî)* and the veil which screens [Him] from cognition, as Ibn al-'Arabi said." *AS* (p. 377 n. 1). This divergent reading shows that some read *mâ* as a pronoun and others as a negative particle. Al-Bayhaqi addresses both explanations as possible readings, depending on the meaning not of *mâ* but of *'amâ'*/*'imâ*.

[95] This is similar to the wording cited by Ibn al-Jawzi in *Daf' Shubah al-Tashbih* (1998 Kawthari repr. p. 48): *mâ tahtahu hawâ' wa lâ fawqahu hawâ'*.

township⟩ (12:82) to mean the people of the township.⁹⁶ This is indicated by his saying: 'His Throne stood over the water.'"⁹⁷

Allah's Establishment Over The Throne *(Istiwâ')*

The meaning of what the Muslims say whereby Allah ⟨established Himself over the Throne⟩⁹⁸ is not that He is in contact with it, nor that He is fixed there *(mutamakkin fîh)*, nor that He is circumscribed *(mutahayyiz)* by any of its directions *(jihât)*. However, He is separate *(bâ'in)* from all of His creation. It is but a report whose terms are ordained and so we say it, at the same time denying any modality *(takyîf)* for it, for ⟨There is nothing whatsoever like unto Him, and He is the All-Hearing, the All-Seeing⟩ (42:11).⁹⁹

Al-Ash'ari said that Allah effected an act pertaining to the Throne, which He named "establishment" *(istiwâ')*. This is like other acts of His such as what He named "sustenance" *(rizq)*, "favor" *(ni'ma)*, and others. Furthermore, He did not give the "establishment" a modality beyond saying it is an attribute of action, because of His statement: ⟨Then He rose over the Throne⟩ (25:59), and the word "then" denotes sequence in time, which is the exclusive province of acts. Also, Allah's acts take place without touch nor motion on His part.

Among the perspicuous scholars, Abu al-Hasan 'Ali ibn Muhammad ibn Mahdi al-Tabari said: "Allah is 'in the heaven above everything and es-

---

⁹⁶This is not found in the published edition of Ibn Sallam's *Gharib al-Hadith* (1:213) which only has: "We only interpreted this hadith according to the words of the Arabs, which are based on reason. However, we do not know how that mist was nor its extent, and Allah knows best." The latter sentence is quoted by Ibn al-Athir in *al-Nihaya*. The gloss of "our Lord" as "the Throne of our Lord" is the explanation favored by Ibn al-Athir in *al-Nihaya* and the *Mu'tazili* al-Zamakhshari in his book *al-Fa'iq fi Gharib al-Hadith* (2:186). Ibn al-Athir also quotes al-Azhari's saying: "We believe in the hadith without qualifying it with any description."
⁹⁷*AS* (p. 374-377); *ASH* (2:233-236). Ibn al-'Arabi in his commentary on the hadith in *'Arida al-Ahwadhi* also states that by the Throne all of creation is meant.
⁹⁸Cf. Qur'an 20:4; 25:59; 7:54; 13:2. See Appendix 5, *"Istiwa'* Is A Divine Act" (p. 87).
⁹⁹*AS* (p. 396-397); *ASH* (2:280).

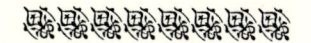

tablished over His Throne' in the sense that He is elevated high *('âlin)* above it, and the sense of *istiwâ'* is elevation *(i'tilâ')*." . . .

The Preternal One *(al-Qadîm)* is thus elevated over His Throne but neither sitting on *(qâ'id)* nor standing on *(qâ'im)* nor in contact with *(mumâss)*, nor separate from *(mubâyin)* the Throne – meaning separate in His Essence in the sense of physical separation or distance. For "contact" and its opposite "separation," "standing" and its opposite "sitting," are all the characteristics of bodies *(ajsâm)*, whereas ⟨**Allah is One, Everlasting, neither begetting nor begotten, and there is none like Him.**⟩ (112:1-4) Therefore what is allowed for bodies is impermissible for Him.

The teacher Abu Bakr ibn Furak also mentioned the above method if interpretation from one of our companions who said: "He established Himself in the sense of elevated." Then he said that such elevation is not in the sense of distance, nor boundary, nor place in which He is firmly fixed. Rather, he means by it what Allah meant when He said: ⟨**Have you taken security from Him Who is in the heaven. . .**⟩ (67:16-17), that is, above it, together with the preclusion of limit *(hadd)* for Him and the fact that He admits neither of being contained by a heavenly stratum nor of being encompassed by an earthly expanse of space. Allah Almighty was described thus in the evidence transmitted, and so we do not dispute what the evidence said.[100]

Allah's Coming *(Ityân)* And Arrival *(Majî')*[101]

Al-Hakim narrated that [the Tabi'i] Abu al-'Aliya said concerning the verse ⟨**Wait they for naught else than that Allah should come unto them in the shadows of the clouds with the angels?**⟩ (2:210): "It means the angels come in the clouds, and Allah comes in whatever He wishes."[102] The

---

[100] *AS* (p. 410-411); *ASH* (2:308-309). Cf. Imam Malik: "He is neither ascribed a limit nor likened with anything" *(lâ yuhaddad wa lâ yushabbah)*. Ibn al-'Arabi said after citing it in *Ahkam al-Qur'an* (4:1740): "This is a pinnacle of *tawhîd* in which no Muslim preceded Malik."
[101] See Appendix 6, "Allah's 'Coming' and 'Arrival'" (p. 95).
[102] Narrated by al-Bayhaqi with a "soft" chain – because of Abu Ja'far al-Razi whom Ibn Hajar declared "credible, but poor in memorizing" – through al-Hakim (*AS* p. 448; *ASH* 2:370 #943), and by al-Tabari, Ibn Abi Hatim, al-Qurtubi, and al-Suyuti in their *Tafsir* (verse 2:210), also by Abu 'Ubayd ibn Sallam and Ibn al-Mundhir as

verse also reads, in one of the Qur'anic readings, ⟨that Allah should come unto them with the angels in the shadows of the clouds.⟩¹⁰³ It is like His saying: ⟨A day when the heaven with the clouds will be rent asunder and the angels will be sent down, a great descent.⟩ (25:25)

The above commentary correctly establishes that the clouds are a place and vehicle only for the angels, whereas there is neither place nor vehicle for Allah Almighty. As for the "coming" and "arrival" [cf. ⟨And your Lord shall arrive with angels, rank on rank⟩ (89:22)]: according to Abu al-Hasan al-Ash'ari, Allah Almighty on the Day of Judgment shall bring about a certain act *(fi'l)* which He named "coming" and "arrival". It does not mean that He moves about *(yataharrak)* or displaces Himself *(yantaqil)*. For movement, stillness, and settlement are among the attributes of bodies, while Allah Almighty is ⟨One, Everlasting⟩ (112:1-2) ⟨and there is nothing whatsoever like unto Him⟩ (42:11).

This is like His saying: ⟨So Allah visited *(atâ)* their building at the foundations, and then the roof fell down upon them from above them, and the doom came *(atâ)* on them whence they knew not.⟩ (16:26) He did not mean a coming of displacement, but only the bringing about of the act whereby their building was destroyed and the oof collapsed on top of them. He named that action "a coming".

Allah's Descent *(Nuzûl)*¹⁰⁴

Al-Ash'ari said the same thing concerning the reports of the "descent" whereby "Allah descends to the nearest heaven in the last third of the night and asks: 'Is anyone asking forgiveness so that I may forgive him?'"¹⁰⁵ Namely, that what is meant thereby is an act brought to be by Allah in the nearest heaven every night, which he named "a descent", without movement

---

stated in Suyuti's *al-Durr al-Manthur*. Al-Kawthari (p. 448) decried Abu al-'Aliya's phrase "and Allah comes in whatever He wishes" as "a condemnable expression."
¹⁰³ As confirmed by al-Qurtubi in his *Tafsir* (verse 2:210). The Qur'anic reading in question is identified as that of Ubayy ibn Ka'b in Suyuti's *Tafsir* for the same verse.
¹⁰⁴ See Appendix 7, "The Hadith of Allah's 'Descent'" (p. 99).
¹⁰⁵ A mass-narrated *(mutawâtir)* report of the Prophet ﷺ in Bukhari and Muslim.

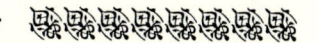

(haraka) nor displacement *(naqla)*. Exalted is Allah above the characteristics of creatures![106]

Allah's Facing Of The Worshipper

Concerning the hadith: "The Prophet ﷺ saw sputum where one faces to pray in the mosque as he was leading the people in prayer. When he terminated the prayer he said: 'Whenever one of you stands to pray, in truth Allah Almighty is before his face *(qibala wajhih)*. Therefore let no-one spit in front of him in prayer.'"[107] Similarly: "The Prophet ﷺ saw sputum where one faces to pray in the mosque which he wiped off with his hand, and the heaviness of the matter showed on his face. He said: 'When the servant prays, he does nothing short of conversing with his Lord' or – the narrator hesitated – 'his Lord is between him and the direction he faces to pray. Therefore, if someone spits, let him do so to his left, or under his foot, or let him do this' –

---

[106] *AS* (p. 447-449); *ASH* (2:370-371). Note that the "Salafi" editor of *al-Asma' wa al-Sifat* takes exception at this negation of movement *(al-haraka)* on Allah's part on the grounds that no text explicitly states such negation *ASH* (2:371, 2:379). Imam al-Kawthari said in his *Maqalat* (350-353): "In *al-Ta'sis fi Radd Asas al-Taqdis* ("The Laying of the Foundation: Refutation of [al-Razi's] *Asas al-Taqdis* ['The Foundation of Declaring Allah's Transcendence']") Ibn Taymiyya says: 'It is well-known that the Book, the Sunna, and the Consensus nowhere say anything to the effect that bodies are all created *(lam tantiq bi anna al-ajsāma kullahā muhdathatun)*, nor that Allah Himself is not a body *(wa annallāha laysa bi jismin)*. None of the imams of the Muslims ever said such a thing. Therefore if I also choose not to say it, it does not expel me from the Religion nor from the Law.' Indeed the above is complete impudence. What did he do with all the verses declaring Allah to be far removed from having anything like unto Him? Does he expect that every absurdity that every idiot can come up with be addressed with a specific text? Is it not enough that Allah the Exalted said: ❨Nothing whatsoever is like unto Him❩ (42:11)? Or does he consider it permissible for someone to say: Allah eats this, and chews this, and tastes that, just because no text mentions the opposite?"

[107] Narrated from Ibn 'Umar by Bukhari and Muslim. Ibn Hajar writes: "Some of the *Mu'tazila* have claimed that Allah was everywhere on the basis of the hadith 'If one of you stands in prayer, let him not spit in front of him for Allah is in front of him.' This is evident ignorance, because the hadith then states that he should spit under his foot, which invalidates their principle. The hadith also constitutes a refutation of those who say that Allah is on the Throne 'in person' *(bi dhātih)*." *Fath al-Bari* (1989 ed. 1:669). By the latter phrase Ibn Hajar, like his Shaykh Zayn al-Din al-'Iraqi in his discussion of the same hadith in *Tarh al-Tathrib* (2:382), meant Ibn 'Abd al-Barr and those who followed his position pertaining to Allah's direction.

and he gestured as if he spat in his garment – 'and then rub together [the folds of his garment].'"¹⁰⁸

Abu Sulayman al-Khattabi said:

The interpretation of "in truth Allah Almighty is before his face" is that the direction which Allah has enjoined upon him to face in prayer is before his face, therefore let him keep it free of sputum. The phrase is elliptical and an example of omission and abridgment, as in Allah's saying: ⟨**And they were made to drink the calf into their hearts**⟩ (2:93), that is: love of the calf; or His saying: ⟨**And ask the township**⟩ (12:82) to mean the people of the township. Examples of this figure of style abound in the Qur'an. That direction is assigned to Allah only in the honorific sense, just as one says: "Allah's House," "Allah's Ka'ba," and other similar examples.

The meaning of "his Lord is between him and the direction he faces to pray" is that his facing the direction of prayer makes his intent arrive to his Lord. By implication, it is as if the object of his intent is between him and his direction of prayer. Consequently the Prophet ﷺ ordered that this direction be kept pure of sputum and the like.

Abu al-Hasan ibn Mahdi [al-Tabari] said, according to what Abu Nasr ibn Qatada wrote me from his book, that the meaning of the Prophet's ﷺ saying "Allah is before his face" is that Allah's reward for that worshipper descends upon him from the direction he is facing. An example for this meaning is his saying: "The Qur'an shall come in front of its companion on the Day of Judgment."¹⁰⁹ That is: the reward of reciting the Qur'an. The following hadith of Abu Dharr confirms this interpretation. The Prophet ﷺ said: "If one of you stands to pray, in truth mercy is facing him."¹¹⁰

---

¹⁰⁸Narrated from Anas by Bukhari.
¹⁰⁹Narrated from Abu Umama by Muslim, Ahmad, Ibn Hibban, al-Hakim and others in the wording: "Recite the Qur'an, for verily, it shall come on the Day of Resurrection as an intercessor for its companions." Also narrated from al-Nawwas ibn Sam'an by Muslim, Ahmad, and al-Tirmidhi: "The Qur'an shall be brought on the Day of Resurrection with its People, those who used to put it into practice, at their vanguard Sura al-Baqara and Al 'Imran."
¹¹⁰Narrated from Abu Dharr in the four *Sunan*, the two *Musnad*s of Ahmad and al-Darimi, and the two *Sahih*s of Ibn Hibban and Ibn Khuzayma. This is a fair *(hasan)*

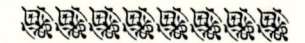

Allah's Face *(Wajh)*

As for Allah's Face, we affirm it as an attribute of Allah, not as a form or image *(sifa lâ min hayth al-sûra)*. About the meaning of the verse ⟪**Wheresoever you turn, there is Allah's countenance**⟫ (2:115) al-Muzani related that al-Shafi'i said it means "the direction which Allah has made you face." Mujahid said: "It is the direction Allah ordered to face for prayer, so that wherever you are, in the East or the West, you must not face other than it."[111] Note that the above verse is abrogated by the verse ⟪**So turn thy face toward the Inviolable Place of Worship**⟫ (2:144) according to Imam Malik.[112]

Allah's Astonishment *('Ajab)* And Laughter *(Dahik)*

It is narrated that the Prophet ﷺ said: "Allah laughs at two men one of whom killed the other, but both enter Paradise. One fights in Allah's cause and is killed, then Allah relents towards the other and guides him to Islam, then he fights in Allah's cause and gets martyred."[113] Abu Sulayman al-Khattabi said concerning the words "Allah laughs":

> There is a kind of laughter which seizes people when joy or amusement overcome them. It is not allowed to apply such laughter

---

narration as stated by al-Tirmidhi and confirmed by Shu'ayb al-Arna'ut in his edition of Ibn Hibban's *Sahih* (6:49-50 #2273-2274), although Ibn Khuzayma declared it sound in his *Sahih* (2:59 #913-914) as well as al-Hakim and al-Dhahabi in the *Mustadrak* (1:236) and Shaykh Ahmad Shakir in his edition of Ahmad's *Musnad* (15:493). 'Abd Allah al-Hashidi contradicted this authentication by ten major hadith masters and two contemporary authorities, declaring the hadith and its chain weak in his edition of Bayhaqi's *al-Asma' wa al-Sifat* (2:90-91 #657, 2:399 #974). Evidently, it does not support "Salafi" doctrine. *AS* (p. 465-466); *ASH* (2:397-399).
[111] *AS* (p. 301, 309); *ASH* (2:81, 2:106-107).
[112] As narrated from Makki by al-Qurtubi in his commentary on the verse. In addition to what al-Bayhaqi stated concerning the Face, it is also established that the *Salaf* interpreted the Face to mean the dominion or sovereignty *(mulk)* in the verse ⟪**Everything will perish save His countenance**⟫ (28:88), as shown by Bukhari's statement in the book of *Tafsir* in his *Sahih*: "Except His *wajh* means except His *mulk*, and it is also said: Except whatever was for the sake of His countenance."
[113] Narrated from Abu Hurayra by Bukhari and Muslim.

to Allah, and it is negated from His Attributes. [His laughter] is but a similitude coined for the deed that counts among human beings as a cause for astonishment, so that when they see it they laugh.[114] Its meaning as Allah's attribute is to inform of His good pleasure as the deed of one of the two men and His acceptance of the other followed by the translation of both to Paradise for what they did, despite the difference in their respective circumstances and intents. Corresponding to the above is what Bukhari narrated whereby someone visited the Prophet ﷺ who said: "Who will host this man?" Whereby one of the *Ansâr* said: "I will." The latter rushed to his wife and told her: "Provide generously for the guest of Allah's Messenger ﷺ." She replied: "We only have the food of the children." He said: "Prepare the food then light the candle and put the children to bed at dinner-time." She did as he said then got up to tinker with light and put it out, and she and her husband pretended to eat but remained hungry that night. The next morning they went to see the Prophet ﷺ and he said: "Last night Allah laughed or was astonished [the narrator hesitated] at what you two did." And Allah revealed the verse: **❰They put others above their need though poverty become their lot❱** (59:9).[115] Al-Bukhari said that the meaning of laughter *(al-dahik)* here is mercy *(al-rahma)*.[116] This interpretation is close to true, and much closer yet, and more probable, is that of good pleasure *(al-rida)*.[117] It is known that laughter on the part of those possessing

---

[114] This is also the definition given by Ibn Qutayba in his *Mukhtalaf al-Hadith* and Abu Bakr ibn al-'Arabi in *al-Qawasim wa al-'Awasim* (2:42). The latter is cited by al-Kawthari's note in *al-Asma' wa al-Sifat* (p. 468-469).
[115] Narrated from Abu Hurayra by Bukhari and Muslim.
[116] Ibn Hajar in *Fath al-Bari* (3:383n.) states that he did not see this in the manuscripts of Bukhari which have reached him, but al-Bayhaqi states that it is narrated from Bukhari by his student al-Farabri. *AS* (p. 298); *ASH* (2:72). Ibn al-Jawzi in *Daf' Shubah al-Tashbih* (1998 Kawthari repr. p. 45-46) explains Allah's laughter as his generosity *(karam)* and favor *(fadl)* while quoting al-Marrudhi's relation from Imam Ahmad that the latter explained Allah's laughter as His abundant generosity *(kathra al-karam)* and vast good pleasure *(si'a al-ridâ)*. Al-Nawawi in *Sharh Sahih Muslim* explains it as a metaphor *(isti'âra)* for good pleasure, bestowal of reward *(thawâb)*, and Allah's love *(mahabba)* according to al-Qadi 'Iyad who added that another possible meaning is that the laughter applies to Allah's angels in charge of seizing the souls of the two men and leading them to Paradise.
[117] This is also the interpretation followed by Ibn Hajar who states in his commentary of the hadith in *Fath al-Bari*: "The attribution of laughter and wonder to Allah is figurative *(majâziyya)* and their meaning is Allah's good pleasure at their deed." The

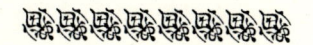

judgment denotes good pleasure and joy. It is the first sign that they accepted the entreaty made to them, the preliminary to the success of the petitioners. Generous and benevolent people, when solicited, are described as showing good humor and amiability.[118] That is also the meaning of "Allah laughs at two men": that is, He lavishes His generosity upon them, for that is the necessary cause of the laughter and its necessary conclusion.[119]

Abu Sulayman said concerning the words "Allah was astonished":

> Concerning the words "Allah was astonished": Astonishment cannot be applied to Allah Almighty nor befits His Attributes. Its significance is only good pleasure, and it actually means that the deed of the two spouses met with Allah's good pleasure, acceptance, and manyfold rewards in the place of something trivial which causes our astonishment for being placed high above its value, and being repaid many times its kind. Its meaning may also be that Allah causes astonishment and laughter among the angels.[120]

"Salafi" commentator 'Abd al-'Aziz Bin Baz reacts by suggesting that al-Bukhari, al-Khattabi, Ibn Hajar etc. "are abandoning the way of the Companions, the Successors, and their excellent followers" and he states: "Would that the author [Ibn Hajar] had cleansed his work from declarations other than the Prophet's ﷺ own declarations." In such obscurantist perspective we should equally "cleanse" all books in Islam of the explanations of the words of Allah and His Prophet. See *Fath al-Bari* (6:50n. book of Jihad Ch. 28 #2826, also 7:151, 8:816).

[118] Ibn al-Jawzi in *Daf' Shubah al-Tashbih* considered it obligatory to interpret Allah's laughter to mean the disclosure of His generosity and of His goodness.

[119] *AS* (p. 469-470); *ASH* (2:401-403). This is also the explanation of Ibn Hajar in *Fath al-Bari* (7:151, 8:816): "Good pleasure on Allah's part necessitates mercy from Him, since the two necessarily go together."

[120] *AS* (p. 470); *ASH* (2:403). The interpretation whereby "Allah causes astonishment and laughter among the angels" is also that of Ibn Hibban in his *Sahih* (10:522) and that of al-Qadi 'Iyad as reported by al-Nawawi in *Sharh Sahih Muslim* (13/14:256). The "Salafi" commentator 'Abd Allah al-Hashidi in his footnote (*ASH* 2:403-404) objects to this interpretation as "null and void and without any rational or textual basis," and he refers the reader to some pages of Ibn Taymiyya's *Fatawa* – an ironic example of the rejection of the *Salaf* for a later author in the name of "Salafism."

Allah's Love *(mahabba)*, Hate *(bughd)*, and Dislike *(karâhiyya)*

Allah said:

- ❨Say: If you love Allah, follow me; Allah will love you❩[121] (3:31)

- ❨Truly Allah loves those who turn unto Him, and loves those who have a care for cleanness❩ (2:222)

- ❨Lo! Allah loves those who battle for His cause in ranks❩ (61:4)

- ❨Allah loves not the utterance of hard speech save by one who has been wronged❩ (4:148)

- ❨Lo! Allah loves not each braggart boaster❩ (31:18)

- ❨And if they had wished to go forth they would assuredly have made ready some equipment, but Allah was averse to their being sent forth and held them back❩ (9:46)

It is mentioned in the hadith that the Prophet ﷺ said:

- "When Allah loves a servant of His He says to Jibril: 'Truly, I love So-and-So, therefore love him too!' Whereupon Jibril says to the inhabitants of the heaven: 'Your Lord loves So-and-So, therefore love him too!' At this all the inhabitants of the heaven love that one, and acceptance is marked for him on earth. If someone is hated, the reverse happens."[122]

- The eve of Khaybar the Prophet ﷺ said: "Tomorrow I shall give the flag to a man at whose hands Allah shall grant us victory, who loves

---

[121] Imam Malik explained this verse to mean: "Whoever loves to obey Allah, He will love him and make him beloved to His creatures." In Makki's *al-Hidaya* (1:39) as quoted in Hamid Lahmar, *al-Imam Malik Mufassir* (p. 131).
[122] Narrated from Abu Hurayra by Bukhari and Muslim. Imam Malik also narrated it in the *Muwatta'*.

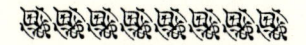

Allah and His Messenger, and whom Allah and His Messenger love." The next day he summoned 'Ali ibn Abi Talib ﷺ.[123]

- "There are two phrases that are light on the tongue, dearest to the Merciful, and heaviest in the Balance: *subhân Allâh wa bi hamdihi, subhân Allâh al-'azîm*."[124]

- "There is no speech dearer to Allah than *al-hamdu lillâh wa subhân Allâh wallâhu akbar wa lâ ilâha illallâh*: they are only four words, so I do not find them too much to say, and it is indifferent whichever you begin with."[125]

- The Prophet ﷺ said to Ashajj 'Abd al-Qays: "There are two traits in you which Allah loves as does His Prophet: forbearance *(al-hilm)* and equanimity *(al-anât)*."[126]

- 'Umar came out to the mosque one day and found Mu'adh ibn Jabal at the grave of the Prophet ﷺ, weeping. He said: "What is causing you to weep, O Mu'adh?" He replied: "What is making me weep is a hadith I heard the Prophet ﷺ say. He said: 'A little self-display constitutes *shirk*, and whoever shows enmity to Allah's Friends has declared war on Allah. Verily, Allah loves the pious, the Godwary in hiding who are not missed when absent nor noticed when present. Their hearts are the lights of guidance. They shall come out of affliction and injustice unscathed.'"[127]

- "Whoever loves to meet Allah, Allah loves to meet him; whoever hates to meet Allah, Allah hates to meet him." 'A'isha or another

---

[123] Narrated by Sahl ibn Sa'd and Abu Hurayra by Bukhari and Muslim.
[124] Narrated from Abu Hurayra by Bukhari and Muslim.
[125] Narrated from Samura ibn Jundub by Muslim.
[126] Narrated from Abu Sa'id al-Khudri by Muslim.
[127] Narrated by al-Tahawi in *Mushkil al-Athar* (2:317) and al-Hakim in the *Mustadrak* (1:4) with a sound *(sahîh)* chain. Ibn Majah, al-Tabarani in *al-Kabir*, and al-Hakim (2:317) also narrate it with a weak chain due to a rejected narrator, 'Isa ibn 'Abd al-Rahman al-Zurqi. The hadith is also narrated from the words: "Allah loves the pious" to the end by Ibn Abi Hatim in his *Tafsir* (verse 58:22) as cited by Ibn Kathir in his; also from Ibn 'Umar by Abu Nu'aym in the *Hilya* (1:46 #25) and al-Hakim (3:270) with a sound *mursal* chain because Abu Qilaba 'Abd Allah ibn Zayd (d. 104-107) did not narrate from Ibn 'Umar.

one of the wives of the Prophet ﷺ said: "We truly hate death!" He replied: "It is not all the same. The believers, when death comes to them, are given the glad tidings of Allah's good pleasure and of His lavish gifts, whereupon they love to meet Him. Whereas the disbeliever, when death comes to them, are given the tidings of Allah's punishment and requital, wheruopon they hate to meet Him."[128]

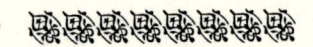

- "Beware, stay away from immorality, for Allah does not like immorality nor immoral acts." It was asked: "O Messenger of Allah, what is the best emigration *(hijra)*?" He replied: "Emigration away from what your Lord abhors."[129]

- "Whoever was given his share of gentle character has received his share of goodness. Whoever was deprived of his share of gentle character was deprived of his share of goodness. The heaviest thing in the Believer's Balance is a good character. Allah truly abhors coarse, indecent persons."[130]

- "Most abhorrent to Allah is the intransigeant, contentious person."[131]

- The Prophet ﷺ said about the *Ansâr*: "None loves them except a believer, and none hates them except hypocrites."[132]

---

[128] Narrated from 'Ubada ibn al-Samit by Bukhari and Muslim.
[129] Narrated from 'Amr ibn al-'As by Ahmad with a fair chain. The first part is also narrated by Muslim.
[130] Narrated from Abu al-Darda' until the second mention of "goodness" by al-Tirmidhi who said it is *hasan sahîh*, and from the words "the heaviest thing" by Ibn Hibban in his *Sahih* where it was declared a sound hadith by Shu'ayb al-Arna'ut (12:506 #5693). Thus the two parts of the hadith are authentic, and al-Hashidi's unqualified statement whereby the hadith has a weak chain, although correct in itself, is misleading (*ASH* 2:464 #1050). Al-Tirmidhi further said the subject-matter is confirmed by 'A'isha's narration in Bukhari and Muslim whereby the Prophet ﷺ said: "Verily Allah is gentle *(rafîq)* and He loves gentleness in every single matter," by Jarir ibn 'Abd Allah's similar narration in Muslim and Abu Dawud, and by Abu Hurayra's narration in Bukhari which adds: "You were all sent to make things easy, not to make things difficult."
[131] Narrated from 'A'isha by Bukhari and Muslim.
[132] Narrated from al-Bara' ibn 'Azib by Bukhari and Muslim.

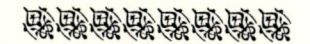

- "There is a kind of mistrust *(ghayra)* which Allah loves and another which Allah hates. [There is a kind of conceit *(khuyalâ')* which Allah loves and another which Allah hates.] The kind of mistrust which Allah loves is mistrust of a doubtful thing *(rîba)*, and the kind that He hates is mistrust in something which is not doubtful. As for the conceit which Allah loves it is the conceit of a combatant when he is fighting. The conceit which Allah hates is a man's pride of himself and arrogance."[133]

Love, hate, and dislike according to some of our [Ash'ari] scholars are among the attributes of acts *(sifât al-fi'l)*. Therefore Allah's love means His praise of someone as embodied by His benevolence towards him, while His hate and dislike mean His blame as embodied by the abasement in which He put him. If praise and blame are through His saying, then His saying is His speech, which is one of His personal attributes *(sifât al-dhât)*. Al-Ash'ari therefore considers that these two go back to His will. Thus Allah's love for the believers goes back to the fact that He wills their benefit and success, while His hatred [goes back to the fact that He means] other than that, that is: His blame of someone's deed goes back to the fact that He wills their humiliation and disgrace. Also, His love of noble qualities goes back to the fact that He wills benevolence towards their owner, while His hatred of despicable qualities goes back to the fact that He wills abasement for their owner, and Allah knows best.[134]

---

[133]Narrated from Jabir ibn 'Atik ibn Qays al-Ansari by Ahmad and al-Tabarani with a sound chain as stated by Haythami in *Majma' al-Zawa'id*; Abu Dawud; al-Tirmidhi who said it is *hasan gharîb*; al-Nasa'i; al-Darimi; al-Hakim (1:418) who said it is *sahîh*; Ibn Hajar in *al-Isaba* (1:216) where he said it is *sahîh*; 'Abd al-Razzaq in his *Musannaf* (10:409) and Ibn Abi Shayba in his (4:420); al-Bayhaqi in his *Sunan*; and Ibn Hibban in his *Sahih*, where Shaykh Shu'ayb al-Arna'ut declared it *hasan*, as did al-Albani in his *Irwa' al-Ghalil* (7:58-60). Opposing all the above, al-Hashidi alone said that the hadith was *da'if* (ASH 2:467-469 #1053).
[134]*AS* (p. 498-502); *ASH* (2:458-470).

Appendix 1

Allah's Beautiful Names

1. *Allâh*

Ism al-Dhât al-Qudsiyya The Name of the Holy Essence
Ism al-Jalâla The Name of Glory
al-Ism al-A'zam The Most Magnificent Name

2. *Al-Rahmân*	The All-Beneficent
3. *Al-Rahîm*	The Most Merciful
4. *Al-Malik*	The King, The Sovereign
5. *Al-Quddûs*	The Most Holy
6. *Al-Salâm*	Peace and Blessing
7. *Al-Mu'min*	The Guarantor
8. *Al-Muhaymin*	The Guardian, the Preserver
9. *Al-'Azîz*	The Almighty, the Self-Sufficient
10. *Al-Jabbâr*	The Powerful, the Irresistible
11. *Al-Mutakabbir*	The Tremendous
12. *Al-Khâliq*	The Creator
13. *Al-Bâri'*	The Maker
14. *Al-Musawwir*	The Fashioner of Forms
15. *Al-Ghaffâr*	The Ever-Forgiving
16. *Al-Qahhâr*	The All-Compelling, the Subduer
17. *Al-Wahhâb*	The Bestower
18. *Al-Razzâq*	The Ever-Providing
19. *Al-Fattâh*	The Opener, the Victory-Giver
20. *Al-Alîm*	The All-Knowing, the Omniscient
21. *Al-Qâbid*	The Restrainer, the Straitener
22. *Al-Bâsit*	The Expansive, the Munificent
23. *Al-Khâfid*	The Abaser
24. *Al-Râfi'*	The Exalter
25. *Al-Mu'izz*	The Giver of Honor

26. *Al-Mudhill*	The Giver of Dishonor
27. *Al-Samî'*	The All-Hearing
28. *Al-Basîr*	The All-Seeing
29. *Al-Hakam*	The Judge, the Arbitrator
30. *Al-'Adl*	The Just
31. *Al-Latîf*	The Subtly Kind
32. *Al-Khabîr*	The All-Aware
33. *Al-Halîm*	The Forbearing, the Indulgent
34. *Al-'Azîm*	The Magnificent, the Infinite
35. *Al-Ghafûr*	The All-Forgiving
36. *Al-Shakûr*	The Grateful
37. *Al-'Aliyy*	The Sublime, the All-High
38. *Al-Kabîr*	The Great
39. *Al-Hafiz*	The Preserver
40. *Al-Muqît*	The Nourisher
41. *Al-Hasîb*	The Reckoner
42. *Al-Jalîl*	The Majestic
43. *Al-Karîm*	The Bountiful, the Generous
44. *Al-Raqîb*	The Watchful
45. *Al-Mujîb*	The Responsive, the Answerer
46. *Al-Wâsi'*	The Vast, the All-Encompassing
47. *Al-Hakîm*	The Wise
48. *Al-Wadûd*	The Loving, the Kind One
49. *Al-Majîd*	The All-Glorious
50. *Al-Bâ'ith*	The Raiser of the Dead
51. *Al-Shahîd*	The Witness
52. *Al-Haqq*	The Truth, the Real
53. *Al-Wakîl*	The Trustee, the Dependable
54. *Al-Qawiyy*	The Strong
55. *Al-Matîn*	The Firm, the Steadfast
56. *Al-Walî*	The Protecting Friend, Patron, and Helper
57. *Al-Hamîd*	The All-Praiseworthy
58. *Al-Muhsî*	The Accounter, the Numberer of All
59. *Al-Mubdi'*	The Producer, Originator, and Initiator of all
60. *Al-Mu'îd*	The Reinstater Who Brings Back All
61. *Al-Muhyî*	The Giver of Life
62. *Al-Mumît*	The Bringer of Death, the Destroyer
63. *Al-Hayy*	The Ever-Living

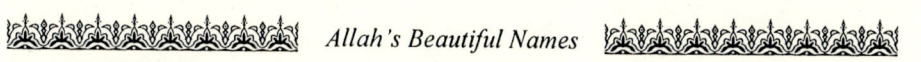

64. Al-Qayyûm	The Self-Sustaining and Sustainer of All
65. Al-Wâjid	The Perceiver, the Finder, the Unfailing
66. Al-Mâjid	The Illustrious, the Magnificent
67. Al-Wâhid	The One, the All-Inclusive, the Indivisible
68. Al-Samad	The Self-Sufficient, the Impregnable, the Eternally Besought of All, the Everlasting
69. Al-Qâdir	The All-Able
70. Al-Muqtadir	The All-Determiner, the Dominant
71. Al-Muqaddim	The Expediter, He who brings forward
72. Al-Mu'akhkhir	The Delayer, He who puts far away
73. Al-Awwal	The First
74. Al-Âkhir	The Last
75. Al-Zâhir	The All-Victorious; the Manifest
76. Al-Bâtin	The All-Encompassing; The Most Hidden
77. Al-Wâli	The Patron
78. Al-Muta'âli	The Highly Exalted, the Transcendent
79. Al-Barr	The Most Kind and Righteous
80. Al-Tawwâb	The Ever-Returning, Ever-Relenting
81. Al-'Afuww	The Pardoner, the Effacer of Sins
82. Al-Muntaqim	The Avenger
83. Al-Ra'ûf	The Compassionate, the All-Pitying
84. Mâlik al-Mulk	The Owner of All Sovereignty
85. Dhu al-Jalâl wa al-Ikrâm	The Lord of Majesty and Generosity
86. Al-Muqsit	The Equitable, the Requiter
87. Al-Jâmi'	The Gatherer, the Unifier
88. Al-Ghanî	The All-Rich, the Independent
89. Al-Mughnî	The Enricher, the Emancipator
90. Al-Mu'tî	The Giver
91. Al-Mâni'	The Withholder, the Shielder, the Defender
92. Al-Nâfi'	The Propitious, the Benefactor
93. Al-Dârr	The Distresser, the Harmer
94. Al-Nûr	The Light
95. Al-Hâdi	The Guide
96. Al-Badî'	The Incomparable, the Originator
97. Al-Bâqi	The Everlasting, the Immutable, the Eternal
98. Al-Wârith	The Heir, the Inheritor of All
99. Al-Rashîd	The Guide, Infallible Teacher, and Knower
100. Al-Sabûr	The Patient, the Timeless

Appendix 2

The Controversy Over The Pronunciation of the Qur'an[135]

Ahl al-Sunna agree one and all that the Qur'an is Allah's pre-existent, pre-eternal, uncreated speech. Imam Malik gave the most succint statement of this doctrine: "The Qur'an is Allah's speech, Allah's speech comes from Him, and nothing created comes from Allah."[136] Where the imams differed was over the pronunciation of the Qur'an. Some, like Bukhari, Muslim, and the entire Ash'ari school, held that the pronunciation was created, while others, like the Hanbalis (other than Imam Ahmad), insisted that the pronunciation was governed by the same belief in uncreatedness as the Qur'an itself.

It is narrated that Muhammad ibn Isma'il al-Sulami heard Imam Ahmad say: "The 'pronunciationists' – those who say that their pronunciation of the Qur'an is created – are Jahmis *(al-lafziyya jahmiyya)*. Allah said: **'Until he hears Allah's speech'** (9:6). From whom does he hear it?"[137] This is similar to the hadith master Musaddad ibn Musarhad al-Asadi's (d. 228) narration from Ahmad with a weak chain: "Whatever is in the volumes of Qur'an *(masâhif)*, whatever recitation is performed by the people, whatever way it is recited, and whatever way it is described: all this is Allah's speech, uncreated. Whoever says it is created is a disbeliever in Allah Almighty; and whoever does not declare him so, is himself a disbeliever! . . . Some of the Jahmis said: 'Our pronunciation of the Qur'an is created': All these are disbelievers."[138]

Despite the apparent authenticity of their transmission, nevertheless the above relations are misleading and most likely inauthentic. Al-Bukhari

---

[135] See al-Buti, *Kubra al-Yaqinat* (p. 126-127). Also see above, al-Bayhaqi's sections entitled "Allah's Speech" (p. 32) and "The Recitation of the Qur'an" (p. 32).
[136] Al-Dhahabi, *Siyar* (7:416).
[137] Narrated with a chain of reliable narrators by Ibn Abi Ya'la in *Tabaqat al-Hanabila* (1:280 #388).
[138] Also in the *Tabaqat* (1:342 #494).

said in *Khalq Afʿal al-ʿIbad*: "As for what the two parties from the school of Ahmad have claimed as proof, each for his own position: Much of what they relate is not established as authentic."[139] Ibn al-Subki said that what was (authentically) related from Imam Ahmad is that he declared as an innovation, not disbelief, al-Karabisi's statement that one's pronunciation of the Qur'an was created *(lafzuka bihi maklûq)*.[140] What reconciles the two views reported from Ahmad is that some may have given his words the most severe meaning possible, namely the sense of a *bidʿa mukaffira* or innovation that constitutes disbelief. Note that it was also al-Karabisi's view that whoever contradicts his statement that one's pronunciation of the Qur'an was created commits disbelief, and so Ahmad did not contradict it, but declared it an innovation instead.

Such doctrines are largely a reaction explained by the charged climate prevalent in Ahmad's time and the sway of the *Jahmiyya* over the caliphate which culminated in the persecution of *Ahl al-Sunna* scholars. At the time of Imam Ahmad's 28-month[141] detention and lashing by the authorities he was pressed to admit to the creation of the Qur'an by the following arguments as narrated by his son Salih ibn Ahmad ibn Hanbal:

> Questioner: What do you say about the Qur'an?
> Ahmad: And you, what do you say about Allah's knowledge?
> Another questioner: Did not Allah say: ❮Allah is the Creator of all things❯ (13:16), and is not the Qur'an a thing?
> Ahmad: Allah also said: ❮Destroying all things❯ (46:25), then it destroyed all except whatever Allah willed.
> Another questioner: ❮Never comes there unto them a new reminder from their Lord❯ (21:2). Can something new be anything but created?
> Ahmad: Allah said: ❮Sâd. By the Qur'an that contains the Reminder.❯ (38:1) "The" reminder is the Qur'an, while the other verse does not say "the".
> Another questioner: But the hadith of ʿImran ibn Husayn states: "Allah created the Reminder."

---

[139] As quoted by al-Kawthari in his edition of *al-Asmaʾ wa al-Sifat* (p. 266).
[140] Ibn al-Subki, *Tabaqat al-Shafiʿiyya* (2:118-119).
[141] Shaykh Shuʿayb Arnaʾut's mention of "ten years" in his introduction to *Sahih Ibn Hibban* (p. 22) is inaccurate.

> Ahmad: That is not correct, several narrated it to us as: "Allah wrote the Reminder."[142]
>
> Then they forwarded the hadith of Ibn Mas'ud: "Allah did not create a garden of Paradise nor a fire of Hell nor a heaven nor an earth more tremendous *(a'zam)* than the verse of the Throne (2:255)."[143]
>
> Ahmad: The creating here applies to the garden, the fire, the heaven, and the earth. It does not apply to the Qur'an.
>
> Another questioner: The narration of Khabbab states: "I admonish you to approach Allah with all that you can; but you can never approach Him with something dearer to Him than His speech."[144]
>
> Ahmad: And that is true.[145]

The Hanbalis sometimes went too far in their reaction, as demonstrated by the boycott of Imam al-Bukhari led by the *Amir al-Mu'minin fi al-Hadith* ("Commander of the Faithful in the Science of Hadith") of Khurasan, Muhammad ibn Yahya al-Dhuhli (d. 258), whom Abu Zur'a ranked above Muslim and who once said: "I have made Ahmad ibn Hanbal an Imam in all that stands between me and my Lord."[146] Al-Dhuhli's boycott led Bukhari's ultimate expulsion from Naysabur for saying something that aroused their suspicion that he was a *Jahmi*![147] Ibn al-Subki relates the incident and elaborates on it:

> Abu Muhammad ibn 'Adi said: "Many shaykhs mentioned to me that when Muhammad ibn Isma'il (al-Bukhari) came to Naysabur and was attended by the throngs of people, some of the shaykhs began to feel jealous of him and said to the authorities in hadith: 'Muhammad

---

[142] Bukhari, *Sahih*, book of the Beginning of Creation: "Allah was when there was nothing else than Him, and His Throne was over the water, and He wrote in the Reminder *(al-dhikr)* all things, and He created the heavens and the earth."
[143] Narrated by Sa'id ibn Mansur, Ibn al-Mundhir, Ibn al-Daris, al-Tabarani, al-Harawi in his *Fada'il*, and al-Bayhaqi in *Shu'ab al-Iman*, as stated by al-Suyuti in *al-Durr al-Manthur*. Al-Tirmidhi in his *Sunan* mentions Sufyan ibn 'Uyayna's explanation whereby this is because the garden, the fire, etc. are all created as opposed to the Qur'an.
[144] Narrated by al-Hakim (2:441) who declared it sound – al-Dhahabi concurred – and by al-Bayhaqi in *al-Asma' wa al-Sifat* with two sound chains (1:587-588 #513-514).
[145] *Siyar A'lam al-Nubala'* (9:478), *Tabaqat al-Shafi'iyya al-Kubra* (2:46-47).
[146] Narrated by al-Dhahabi in the *Siyar* (10:205).
[147] Cf. al-Dhahabi, *Siyar* (10:207, 10:311-316).

'Muhammad ibn Isma'il says: "The pronouncing of the Qur'an is created," so investigate him.' When the people gathered, one man got up and asked him: 'O Abu 'Abd Allah, what do you say about pronouncing the Qur'an, is it created or uncreated?' He ignored him and did not reply, so the man repeated the question, so he ignored him again, so he repeated it again, at which point Bukhari turned to him and said: 'The Qur'an is Allah's speech and is uncreated; the actions of servants are created; and investigating someone is an innovation.' At this the man cried out, there was a general uproar, the crowd dispersed, and Bukhari sat alone in his house."

Muhammad ibn Yusuf al-Farabri said: I heard Muhammad ibn Isma'il say: "As for the actions of servants, they are created: 'Ali ibn 'Abd Allah narrated to us: Marwan ibn Mu'awiya narrated to us: Abu Malik narrated to us from Rib'i from Hudhayfa who said that the Prophet ﷺ said: 'Truly, Allah makes every maker and his making.' *(innallâha yasna'u kulla sâni'in wa san'atahu.)*[148] And I heard 'Ubayd Allah ibn Sa'id say: I heard Yahya ibn Sa'id say: I can still hear our companions saying: 'Truly, the actions of servants are created.'

Al-Bukhari continued: "Their motions *(harakât)*, voices *(aswât)*, earning *(iktisâb)*, and writing *(kitâba)* are created. As for the Qur'an that is declaimed *(matluw)*, established *(muthbat)* in the volumes, inscribed *(mastûr)*, written *(maktûb)*, contained *(mû'a)* in the hearts: that is Allah's speech, uncreated. Allah said: **'But it is clear revelations in the hearts of those who have been given knowledge.'** (29:49) [Bayhaqi's narration in *al-Asma' wa al-Sifat* (2:7 #570) adds: al-Bukhari said: Ishaq ibn Ibrahim said: "As for the containers, who doubts that they are created?"]

"It is said: 'So-and-so's recitation is excellent,' and 'So-and-so's recitation is bad.' It is not said: 'His Qur'an is excellent' or 'His Qur'an is bad.' And to the servants is the recitation attributed, for the Qur'an is Allah's speech, while the recitation is the act of the servant, and no-one can legislate concerning Allah without knowledge unlike

---

[148]Narrated by al-Bukhari in *Khalq Af'al al-'Ibad*, al-Bayhaqi in *al-Asma' wa al-Sifat* with three sound chains and in the *Shu'ab*, and al-Hakim in *al-Mustadrak* with a sound *(sahîh)* chain as confirmed by al-Dhahabi.

some have claimed when they said that the Qur'an is one with our pronouncing it, that our pronouncing it is one thing together with it, that declamation *(al-tilâwa)* is itself the thing declaimed *(al-matluw)*, and recitation *(al-qirâ'a)* is itself the thing recited *(al-maqrû')*. Such a one must be told: declamation is the act of the reciter and the deed of the one declaiming."

Abu Hamid al-A'mashi said: "I saw al-Bukhari at the funeral of Sa'id ibn Marwan, at which time al-Dhuhli was asking him about the names and patronyms [of narrators] and the defects [of narrations], and al-Bukhari was going through them like an arrow. Not a month passed after that but al-Dhuhli told us: 'Whoever goes to his gathering, let him not come to ours. They wrote to us from Baghdad that he spoke about pronuncia-tion [of the Qur'an], and we ordered him to stop, which he did not, therefore do not go near him.'" It had been related from Bukhari that he had said: My pronunciation of the Qur'an is created, while al-Dhuhli had said: "Whoever claims that his pronunciation of the Qur'an is created, he is an innovator whose company must be shunned, and whoever claims that the Qur'an is created has committed disbelief."

Muhammad ibn Yahya only meant – and Allah knows best – what Ahmad ibn Hanbal meant, namely to forbid from entering into that subject. He did not mean to contradict Bukhari. If he did mean to contradict him and to claim that the pronunciation which comes out of his own created lips is preternal, that would be an enormity. One would like to believe that he meant other than that and that both he, Ahmad ibn Hanbal, and other imams only meant to prohibit people from entering into problems of *kalâm* (dialectic theology). For us, Bukhari's words are to be understood as a permission to mention *kalâm* if needed, since the use of *kalâm* out of necessity is an obligation *(wâjib)*, while keeping silence about *kalâm* in other than necessity is a *sunna*.[149]

---

[149]This position is reiterated by Ibn al-Subki's younger contemporary al-Shatibi (d. 790) in his book *al-Muwafaqat* (2:332): "Malik ibn Anas used to say: 'I detest talking about Religion, just as the people of our country [al-Madina] detest and prohibit it, in the sense of Jahm's doctrine, *qadar*, and the like. I do not like to speak except about what relates to practice. As for talk about the Religion, I prefer to keep silent about it.' The Congregation of [Sunni] Muslims follow Imam Malik's position, except if

Understand this well, and leave the rantings of historians, and ignore once and for all the distortions of the misguided who think that they are scholars of hadith and that they are standing on the Sunna when in fact they could not be further from it. How could anyone possibly think that Bukhari has anything in common with the position of the *Mu'tazila* when it has been authentically reported from him by al-Farabri and others that he said: "I consider as ignorant whoever does not declare the Jahmis to be disbelievers"? The impartial observer will not doubt that Muhammad ibn Yahya al-Dhuhli suffered from envy, from which none is safe except those who are immune to sin. Some even asked Bukhari about him and he said: "How can envy concerning learning possess Muhammad ibn Yahya, when learning is Allah's wealth which He gives whomever He pleases?"

Bukhari gave a sample of his great intelligence when in reply to Abu 'Amr al-Khaffaf who said to him: People are examining your words "My pronunciation of Qur'an is created" Bukhari said: "O Abu 'Amr, remember what I say to you: Whoever claims, among the people of Naysabur, Qamus, Rayy, Hamadhan, Baghdad, Kufa, Basra, Mecca, and Madina, that I ever said: 'My pronunciation of Qur'an is created,' he is a liar; truly I never said it. All I said is: The actions of servants are created."

Observe his words well and see how intelligent he is! Its meaning is – and Allah knows best: "I did not say that my pronunciation of Qur'an is created for to say such would constitute entering into problematics of dialectical theology and of the attributes of Allah wherein it is unfitting to enter except due to necessity; what I said is: the actions of servants are created, and it is a general foundation which exempts one from mentioning the problematics specifically. For every rational person understands that our pronunciation is part of our actions, and our actions are created, therefore our pronunciation is created."

---

one is obliged to speak. One must not remain silent if his purpose is to refute falsehood and guide people away from it, or if one fears the spread of misguidance or some similar danger."

He has made this meaning explicit in another sound narration reported from him by Hatem ibn Ahmad ibn al-Kindi who said: I heard Muslim ibn al-Hajjaj say – and he recounted the narration in which is the following: "A man stood before Bukhari and asked him about the pronunciation of Qur'an, and he replied: 'Our actions are created, and our pronunciation is part of our actions.'" The story also mentions that the people at that time differed concerning Bukhari, some saying that he had said: My pronunciation of Qur'an is created, others denying it. I say: The only ones to blame are those who indulge in discourse concerning the Qur'an.

In conclusion we repeat what we said in the biography of al-Karabisi:[150] Ahmad ibn Hanbal, and others of the masters of learning to whom Allah has granted success, forbade people to discourse concerning Qur'an although they did not differ (with Bukhari) on the question of pronunciation. This is what we believe about them with due respect for them, based on their sayings in other narrations, and in order to exonerate them from saying something which neither reason nor transmitted evidence support. Furthermore, al-Karabisi, Bukhari, and others of the imams to whom Allah has granted success have made it explicit that their pronunciation is created when they felt the necessity to make it explicit, if it is established that they actually took such an explicit position.[151] We have otherwise brought to the reader Bukhari's saying that whoever relates that he said such a thing, he has reported something false from him.

The reader may ask: If it is the truth then why did he not say it explicitly? I answer: Glory to Allah! We have told you that the gist of this matter is their insistence prohibiting discussions of dialectical theology lest such discussions take them to unseemly consequences. Not every science can be explicited, therefore remember what we impart to you and hold on to it tightly.

I like what Ghazali quotes in *Minhaj al-'Abidin* attributing it to a member of the Prophet's House, Zayn al-'Abidin 'Ali ibn al-Husayn ibn 'Ali:

---

[150] See *Tabaqat al-Shafi'iyya* (2:118-120).
[151] Such as al-Harith al-Muhasibi, Muhammad ibn Nasr al-Marwazi, Muslim ibn al-Hajjaj, and Ahmad ibn Salama.

> *I keep the jewels of my knowledge concealed*
> *Lest the ignorant see Truth and turn away.*
> *How many an essential knowledge, if I divulged it,*
> *I would be told for it: You are of the idol-worshippers;*
> *And righteous men would deem licit my blood*
> *And think well of the ugly deed they would commit.*
> *This is what Abu al-Hasan ('Ali) had already*
> *Advised al-Husayn and, before him, al-Hasan.*[152]

The position that was finally retained by the Hanbali school on the question is less extreme, as shown by Ibn Qudama's (d. 620) statement on the subject:

> Part of Allah's speech is the noble Qur'an, Allah's Book that clarifies all, His firm rope, His straight path, the revelation of the Lord of the worlds. The faithful Spirit brought it down to the heart of the master of Messengers in a clear Arabic tongue. It is revealed, not created, from Him [Allah] did it issue and to Him it shall return. It consists in precise suras, clear verses, letters and words. Whoever recites it *(qara'ahu)* and pronounces it clearly and distinctly *(a'rabahu)* shall receive ten blessings for every letter. It has a beginning and an end, sections and parts. It is recited *(matluwwun)* with the tongues, preserved in the breasts, heard with the ears, written in the volumes. It comprises the precise and the ambiguous, the abrogating and the abrogated, the specific and the general, the command and the prohibition. **'No falsehood can approach it from before or behind it: it is sent down, by One Full of Wisdom, worthy of all Praise'** (41:42). **'Say: if the whole of mankind and Jinns should assemble to produce the like of this Qur'an, they could not produce the like thereof, even if they backed up each other with help and support'** (17:88).[153]

Another authoritative statement of the Sunni doctrine on the topic is given by Taj al-Din Ibn al-Subki:

---

[152] Ibn al-Subki, *Tabaqat al-Shafi'iyya al-Kubra* (2:228-231).
[153] Ibn Qudama, *Lam'a al-I'tiqad* (p. 17 #13).

The Qur'an itself is really written in the volumes *(al-masâhif)*, preserved in the hearts of the believers, read and recited in reality with the tongues of the reciters among the Muslims, just as Allah Almighty is really, and not metaphorically, worshipped in our mosques, known in our hearts, and mentioned with our tongues. This is clear, with Allah's grace and thanks to Him. Whoever deviates from this path is an 'isolationist' proponent of absolute free will *(qadarî mu'tazilî)*.[154]

Of note is Ibn al-Subki's sharp contradiction of the image given by Ibn Abi Ya'la of Imam Ahmad, and Ibn al-Subki's twofold denial: first, that Imam Ahmad ever considered the doctrine that pronunciation is created as disbelief; second, that he ever held that the pronunciation of the Qur'an was uncreated.[155] Al-Dhahabi's position, on the other hand, is to ascribe both views to Imam Ahmad.[156] At the same time he admits, in somewhat circuitous fashion, the difference between pronunciation *(al-talaffuz)* and its content *(al-malfûz)*, recitation *(qirâ'a)* and its content *(al-maqrû')*, and the contingent *(muhdath)* nature of pronunciation, voice *(al-sawt)*, movement *(al-haraka)*, and utterance *(al-natq)*, although loath to admit frankly that they are created.[157] The only possible exception is in al-Dhahabi's notice on Al-Ash'ari's companion, the Shafi'i scholar al-Karabisi.[158] When al-Karabisi heard that Imam Ahmad had declared his statement an innovation whereby the pronunciation of the Qur'an was created, he said: "Pronunciation means other than the thing pronounced" *(talaffuzuka ya'ni ghayra al-malfûz)*. Then he said of Ahmad: "What shall we do with this boy? If we say 'created' he says *bid'a*, and if we say 'not created' he says *bid'a*." Al-Dhahabi commented: "There is no doubt that what al-Karabisi innovated and explained in the question of the pronunciation is the truth, but Imam Ahmad refused it in order to preclude the extension of the question to the Qur'an itself, since one cannot distinguish the pronunciation from the pronounced, which is Allah's speech, except in the mind."

Al-Dhahabi considers that at the root of the disagreement lay a strict refusal, on the part of Imam Ahmad's circle, to countenance any concession

---

[154]Ibn al-Subki, *Tabaqat al-Shafi'iyya al-Kubra* (3:418).
[155]In the *Tabaqat al-Shafi'iyya* (2:118-120).
[156]*Siyar* (9:503-505).
[157]*Siyar* (9:505).
[158]Al-Dhahabi, *Siyar* (10:81-82 #1988).

to what they considered dialectic theology *(kalâm)* and therefore innovation. This attitude was not shared by al-Bukhari and Muslim among others:

> Al-Dhuhli was fierce *(shadîd)* in his adhesion to the Sunna. He confronted Muhammad ibn Isma'il [al-Bukhari] because the latter had alluded, in his *Khalq Af'al al-'Ibad*, to the fact that the reader's utterance of the Qur'an was created. Bukhari made it understood without explicitly saying it, but he certainly made it clear. On the other hand Ahmad ibn Hanbal flatly refused to explore the question, as well as Abu Zur'a and al-Dhuhli, or indulge in the terminology of dialectic theologians *(al-mutakallimûn)*, and they did well – may Allah reward them excellently. Ibn Isma'il had to travel from Naysabur under cover, and he was pained by what Muhammad ibn Yahya [al-Dhuhli] had done to him.[159]
>
> Among those who narrated from al-Dhuhli is Muhammad ibn Isma'il al-Bukhari [34 hadiths according to Ibn Hajar in *Tahdhib al-Tahdhib* 9:516], but he conceals his name a lot *(yudallisuhu kathiran)*. He does not name him "Muhammad ibn Yahya" but only "Muhammad," or "Muhammad ibn Khalid," or "Muhammad ibn 'Abd Allah," linking him to his great-grandfather [and grandfather respectively] and obscuring his name because of the incident that took place between them.[160]
>
> Al-Hakim [narrated with his chains]: Muhammad ibn Yahya [al-Dhuhli] said: "This Bukhari has openly subscribed to the doctrine of 'pronunciationists' *(al-lafziyya)*, and for me those are worse than the *Jahmiyya*." . . . Ahmad ibn Salama visited Bukhari and told him: "O Abu 'Abd Allah, this is a respected man [i.e. al-Dhuhli] in Khurasan, especially in this town [Naysabur], and he has thundered with this speech until none of us can say anything to him about it, so what do you think we should do?" Bukhari grasped his beard then he said: ⟨I confide my cause unto Allah. Lo! Allah is Seer of His slaves.⟩ (40:44) He continued: "O Allah! You know that I did not want for one moment to settle in Naysabur out of arrogance, nor in quest of leadership, but only because my soul would not let me return to my own country [Bukhara] because of my opponents; and now this

---

[159] Al-Dhahabi, *Siyar* (10:207).
[160] Al-Dhahabi, *Siyar* (10:201).

man intends harm for me out of jealousy, only because of what Allah gave me and for no other reason." Then he said to me: "O Ahmad, tomorrow I shall leave and you will be rid of his talk which I caused." . . . Muhammad ibn Ya'qub the hadith master said: "When al-Bukhari settled in Naysabur Muslim ibn al-Hajjaj took to visiting him frequently. When the affair of the pronunciation of Qur'an took place between al-Bukhari and [al-Dhuhli] and the latter roused people against him and forbade them to visit him, most people stopped visiting him, but not Muslim.[161] Then al-Dhuhli said: 'Anyone that subscribes to the pronunciation [being created], it is not permitted for them to attend our gathering.' Whereupon Muslim placed a cloak on top of his turban, stood up in front of everyone, and sent back to al-Dhuhli what he had written from him carried by a camel-driver, for Muslim openly subscribed to the pronunciation and made no attempt to conceal it." . . . Ahmad ibn Mansur al-Shirazi also narrated it from Muhammad ibn Ya'qub, adding: "And Ahmad ibn Salama stood up and followed him."[162]

The Ash'ari view concerning the *maktûb* or content of writing is the same as al-Bukhari's, as shown by Bayhaqi's expression in *al-Asma' wa al-Sifat* (1:478, 2:125): "The *maktûb* is Allah's speech and one of His attributes inseparable from Him."

What possibly reconciles the different views on this subject is that *lafz* is used by some to mean the revealed, uncreated words and contents of recitation, while others mean thereby the mere act of pronunciation, which is created; hence the extreme caution shown by some, such as Imam al-Bukhari, who fell short of saying: "My *lafz* is created" even though he used it in the second sense, since he said: "*Lafz* is an act of human beings, and our acts are created." This lexical ambiguity is a proof of sorts that the differences on this particular question were largely in terminology rather than essence. Added to this is a fundamental difference in method around the appropriateness of such dialectic, which poisoned the air with unnecessary condemnations on the part of Imam Ahmad's followers – and Allah knows best.

---

[161] Nor the imam and hadith master of Khurasan: al-Husayn ibn Muhammad ibn Zyad, Abu 'Ali al-Naysaburi al-Qabbani (d. 289), whom al-Hakim described as "One of the pillars of hadith and of hadith masters in the world." Dhahabi, *Siyar* (11:51f.).
[162] Al-Dhahabi, *Siyar* (10:314-315). Cf. *ASH* (2:20-21 #591).

We did not detail this obsolete page of history except by way of explanation for al-Bayhaqi's text and to show that even the greatest scholars were liable to treat each other unfairly due to misunderstandings. In some of these questions it is obvious that many originally justifiable positions from Imam Ahmad took a life of their own to crystallize into extreme statements and even grave errors at the hands of his epigones. Those errors generally bear the stamp of literalism, and are being propagated in one form or another today by certain parties less knowledgeable than the scholars of the past by far. Their aberrant doctrines are detailed in other publications of Al-Sunna Foundation such as Shaykh Muhammad Hisham Kabbani's *Islamic Beliefs and Doctrine According to Ahl al-Sunna, The Doctrine of Ahl al-Sunna Versus the "Salafi" Movement,* and the *Encyclopedia of Islamic Doctrine.*[163]

---

[163] See also Shaykh 'Abd al-Fattah Abu Ghudda's monograph entitled *Mas'alat Khalq al-Qur'an wa Atharuha fi Sufuf al-Riwat wa al-Muhaddithin wa Kutub al-Jarh wa al-Ta'dil* ("The Question of the Createdness of the Qur'an and its Scathing Effect on the Ranks of the Narrators and Hadith Scholars As Well As on the Books of Narrator-Authentication").

Appendix 3

The Vision of Allah in the World and the Hereafter

Ibn Khafif stated in his *al-'Aqida al-Sahiha*:

30. The believers shall see Allah on the Day of Resurrection just as they see the full moon on the nights when it rises. They will not be unfairly deprived of seeing Him.

31. They will see Him without encompassment *(ihâta)* nor delimitation *(tahdîd)* within any given limit *(hadd)*, whether from the front, the back, above, below, right, or left. ...

97. Sight in the world is impossible.[164]

The *Mu'tazila* and some other groups held that Allah could not be seen at all, even on the Day of Resurrection. They rejected the sound hadiths to the contrary, claiming that such vision necessitated corporeality and direction, which were precluded for Him. *Ahl al-Sunna* adduced the verse ⟪**That day will faces be resplendent, Looking toward their Lord**⟫ (75:22-23) and the mass-narrated hadiths to the effect that such vision will be real. In contrast to the *Mu'tazila*, the totality of the scholars of *Ahl al-Sunna* both excluded modalities of encompassment, delimitation, direction, and other corporeal qualities and, at the same time, held that Allah will be seen by the believers in the Hereafter without specifying how. However, they differed whether such unqualified sight was possible in the world as well.

Al-Qari and al-Haytami reported that the agreement of *Ahl al-Sunna* is that sight of Allah in the world is possible but that it does not take place (except for the Prophet ﷺ), while two contrary opinions on the topic are narrated from al-Ash'ari in al-Qushayri's *Risala*.[165] The proof that His sight is

---

[164]In Shatta, *Sira Ibn Khafif* p. 340-365, translated in full in a separate publication.
[165]Al-Qari, *al-Mirqat* (1892 ed. 5:303); al-Haytami, *Fatawa Hadithiyya* (p. 147-150). The latter said (p. 150): "If it is authenticated that al-Ash'ari held that the vision does

possible in the world was adduced from Musa's ﷺ request to Allah: ⟪My Lord! Show me Your Self, that I may gaze upon You⟫ (7:143) as Prophets do not ask the impossible.[166] Imam al-Qushayri stated in the *Risala* that sight of Allah in the world does not take place for anyone except the Prophet ﷺ while al-Dhahabi, conceding that sight of Allah in the world is possible, held that it does not take place even for the Prophet ﷺ.[167] These views are based on the Prophet's ﷺ hadith: "Verily, you shall not see Allah until you die."[168] Ibn Hajar adduced the hadith: "Worship Allah as if you see Him" as further proof that there is no sight of Allah with the eyes of the head in this world but added: "The Prophet's ﷺ sight of Allah is supported by other evidence."[169]

The Prophet ﷺ saw Allah before death as is the doctrine of the majority of *Ahl al-Sunna* thus related from al-Nawawi by al-Qari.[170] The evidence for this is the hadith of Ibn 'Abbas whereby the Prophet ﷺ said: "I saw my Lord" *(ra'aytu rabbî)*.[171] Ibn Kathir cited it in his commentary on Sura al-Najm and declared its chain sound, but considered it part of the hadith of the dream cited below. Ibn al-Qayyim states that Imam Ahmad considered such sight to be in the Prophet's ﷺ sleep but remains a true sight – as the dreams

---

take place in the world, then that position is ignored as he either did not know of the Consensus to the contrary, or took an anomalous *(shâdhdh)* stance which cannot be taken into consideration."

[166] As stated by al-Qari in *Sharh al-Fiqh al-Akbar*.
[167] In the *Siyar* (8:430-431).
[168] Narrated from Abu Umama ibn al-Samit al-Bahili as part of a longer hadith by Ahmad with a sound chain, as stated by al-Zayn, in the *Musnad* (16:415 #22663), Ibn Majah, al-Nasa'i in *al-Sunan al-Kubra* (4:419 #7764), al-Hakim (4:456) who stated that it is *sahîh* and al-Dhahabi concurred, Ibn Abi 'Asim in *al-Ahad wa al-Mathani* (2:446 #1249) and *al-Sunna* (p. 186-187 #429) with a sound chain as stated by al-Albani, al-Ajurri in *al-Shari'a*, and Ibn Khuzayma in *al-Tawhid*. It is also narrated without mention of the Companion's name by Muslim in his *Sahih*, al-Tirmidhi who declared it *hasan sahih*, Ahmad with a sound chain (17:72 #23562), and Ibn Abi 'Asim in *al-Sunna* (p. 187 #430) with a sound chain.
[169] In *Fath al-Bari* (1959 ed. 1:125 #50).
[170] In *al-Mirqat* (5:308).
[171] Narrated by Ahmad with two chains of which one is sound, and al-Ajurri with a sound chain as stated by the editors of the former's *Musnad* (3:165 #2580, 3:184 #2634) and the latter's *al-Shari'a* (p. 495 #1047) as well as al-Haythami in *Majma' al-Zawa'id* (1:78-79). Also narrated by Ibn Abi 'Asim in *al-Sunna* (p. 188 #433) with the same chain as the second of Imam Ahmad's two narrations. Ahmad and Abu Zur'a considered this hadith authentic, as stated in *Tabaqat al-Hanabila* (1:312, 1:242), al-Suyuti's *al-La'ali* (1:29-30), and al-Diya' al-Maqdisi's *al-Mukhtara* (1:79 #66).

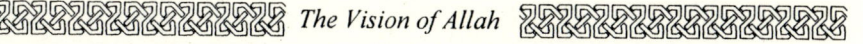

of Prophets are true – and he adds that some of the Imam's companions mistakenly attributed to him the position that the Prophet ﷺ saw his Lord "with the eyes of his head."[172]

Al-Bayhaqi also narrated the hadith "I saw my Lord" in *al-Asma' wa al-Sifat* with a sound chain but with the addition: "in the form of a curly-haired, beardless young man wearing a green robe," a condemned, disauthenticated addition and concatenation with another hadith that refers to Jibril عليه السلام.[173] Hence al-Suyuti interpreted it either as a dream or, quoting his shaykh Ibn al-Humam, as "the veil of form" *(hijâb al-sûra)*.[174]

The latter explanation is echoed in al-Qari's several commentaries of the similar hadith whereby the Prophet ﷺ said: "My Lord came to me in the best form – the narrator said: I think he said: 'in my sleep' – and asked me over what did the Higher Assembly *(al-mala' al-a'lâ)*[175] vie, and I said I did not know, so He put His hand between my shoulders, and I felt its coolness in my innermost, and knowledge of all things between the East and the West came to me."[176]

---

[172] Ibn al-Qayyim, *Zad al-Ma'ad* (3:34).
[173] *AS* (p. 444-445), *ASH* (2:363-364 #938). A "condemned" *(munkar)* narration according to Imam Ahmad as stated in al-Dhahabi's *Tartib al-Mawdu'at* (p. 22 #22), and according to al-Ahdab in *Zawa'id Tarikh Baghdad* (8:37-40 #1662). Ibn al-Jawzi in *Daf' Shubah al-Tashbih* (1998 Kawthari repr. p. 34) states that the hadith is narrated through Hammad ibn Salama and that his foster-son the *zindîq* Ibn Abi al-'Awja' used to interpolate this kind of baseless narrations into his books. Al-Dhahabi also states that it is *munkar* in the *Siyar* (8:430-431), however, he seems to apply this condemnation to the entirety of the narrations in this chapter.
[174] In *al-La'ali' al-Masnu'a* (1:29-30).
[175] I.e. "the angels brought near" according to Ibn al-Athir in *al-Nihaya* and others.
[176] Narrated by al-Tirmidhi with three chains, all *sahîh* according to al-Albani: two from Ibn 'Abbas – in the first of which he said "the knowledge of all things in the heaven and the earth" while he graded the second *hasan gharîb* – and one chain from Mu'adh *(hasan sahîh)* which explicitly mentions that this took place in the Prophet's ﷺ sleep. Al-Bukhari declared the latter chain *sahîh* as stated by al-Tirmidhi in his *Sunan* and in his *'Ilal*, and it towers over all other chains, according to Ibn Hajar in *al-Isaba* (2:397), in the facts that there is no discrepancy over it among the hadith scholars and its text is undisputed (cf. *ASH* 2:78). Also narrated by Ahmad with four sound chains according to Shakir and al-Zayn: one from Ibn 'Abbas with the words "I think he said: 'in my sleep'" (3:458 #3484); one from Mu'adh which Ahmad explicitly declared *sahîh* as narrated by Ibn 'Adi in *al-Kamil* (6:2244), with the words: "I woke up and lo! I was with my Lord" (16:200 #22008); and two from unnamed Companions in which no mention is made of the Prophet's ﷺ sleep or

The Vision of Allah

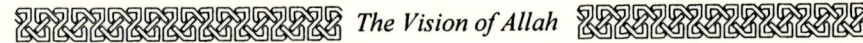

Al-Mubarakfuri relates from Ibn Kathir and al-Haytami the position that the above vision took place in the Prophet's ﷺ sleep. This is also the position of Ibn al-Jawzi based on what he termed the best chains of this hadith.[177] Al-Haytami points out that the words "I woke up and saw my Lord" in Ahmad's narration from Mu'adh are actually changed from "I dozed off and saw my Lord" due to a copyist's corruption of "I dozed off" *(istathqaltu)* – as in al-Tirmidhi's report from Mu'adh – into "I woke up" *(istayqaztu)*.[178] On the whole, the scholars' interpretations of the Prophet's ﷺ vision show that whether it took place in his dream or in a wakeful state, "with the eyes of

---

wakefulness (13:93-94 #16574, 16:556 #23103). Al-Haytami declared the latter sound as well as other chains cited by al-Tabarani in *al-Kabir* (20:109 #216, 20:141 #290) and al-Bazzar in his *Musnad*, and he declared fair the chain narrated from Abu Umama by al-Tabarani in *al-Kabir* (8:290 #8117). See *Majma' al-Zawa'id* (7:176-179). Shaykhs 'Abd al-Qadir and Shu'ayb al-Arna'ut both declared *sahih* the seven narrations of al-Tirmidhi and Ahmad in their edition of Ibn al-Qayyim's *Zad al-Ma'ad* (3:33-34 n. 4). Also narrated from Jabir ibn Samura by Ibn Abi 'Asim in *al-Sunna* (p. 203 #465) with a fair chain according to al-Albani. Also narrated from 'Abd al-Rahman ibn 'A'ish by al-Darimi in his *Musnad* (2:170 #2149) and al-Tabarani through two chains in *al-Ahad wa al-Mathani* (5:48-50 #2585-2586) and another in *Musnad al-Shamiyyin* (1:339 #597), and from Umm al-Tufayl by al-Tabarani in *al-Ahad* (6:158 #3385). The latter chain actually states: "I saw my Lord in the best form of a beardless young man" and was rejected by al-Dhahabi in *Tahdhib al-Mawdu'at* (p. 22 #22). Also narrated from the Companion Abu Rafi' [*al-Isaba* 7:134 #9875] by al-Tabarani in *al-Kabir* (1:317 #938). Also narrated from Ibn 'Abbas by Abu Ya'la in his *Musnad* (4:475 #2608). Some fair narrations of this hadith – such as al-Tabarani's from 'Abd al-Rahman ibn 'Iyash and al-Khatib's from Abu 'Ubayda ibn al-Jarrah in *Tarikh Baghdad* (8:151) – have the words: "I saw my Lord" instead of "My Lord came to me," hence Ibn Kathir's conclusion previously cited. Al-Ahdab in *Zawa'id Tarikh Baghdad* (6:251-253) and al-Haytami also cited Abu 'Ubayda ibn al-Jarrah, Ibn 'Umar, Abu Hurayra, Anas, Thawban, and Abu Umama which brings to at least eleven (without Umm al-Tufayl) the number of Companions who narrated this hadith. The various chains and narrations of this hadith were collated and discussed by Ibn Rajab in his monograph *Ikhtiyar al-Awla fi Sharh Hadith Ikhtisam al-Mala' al-A'la*, ed. Jasim al-Dawsari (Kuwait: Dar al-Aqsa, 1406). See also: Ibn Athir, *Jami' al-Usul* (9:548-550). Among those that considered this hadith as falling below the grade of *sahih* are al-Bayhaqi in *al-Asma' wa al-Sifat* (AS p. 300, ASH 2:72-79), Ibn al-Jawzi in *al-'Ilal al-Mutanahiya* (1:34), Ibn Khuzayma in *al-Tawhid* (p. 214-221) and al-Daraqutni in his *'Ilal* (6:56). Some went too far and suggested that it was forged: see al-Saqqaf, *Aqwal al-Huffaz al-Manthura li Bayan Wad' Hadith Ra'aytu Rabbi fi Ahsani Sura*, appended to his edition of Ibn al-Jawzi's *Daf' Shubah al-Tashbih*.

[177] In *Daf' Shubah al-Tashbih* (Kawthari ed. p. 32).
[178] In Al-Mubarakfuri *Tuhfa al-Ahwadhi* (9:74).

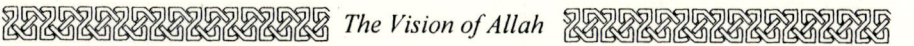

the heart" or "with the eyes of the head," does not change the fact that he saw Him in the real sense, as the Prophet's dream-vision or heart-vision is by far sharper, more accurate, and more real than the visions of ordinary people.

Ahl al-Sunna scholars gave many interpretations of the above hadith. For example, al-Razi and, before him, al-Bayhaqi, interpreted the placing of Allah's Hand as His extreme consideration and attention to the Prophet ﷺ, or as His immense favor to him, while its specific placing between his shoulders refers to the pouring of divine kindness and mercy into his heart, and the coolness refers to the completion and perfection of his knowledge as shown by his words "I knew all things between the East and the West."[179] Al-Qari wrote the following in the chapter on the Prophet's ﷺ turban in his book *Jam' al-Wasa'il fi Sharh al-Shama'il*, a commentary on al-Tirmidhi's *Shama'il* or "Characteristics of the Prophet":

> Whether the Prophet ﷺ saw his Lord in his sleep or whether Allah the Glorious and Exalted manifested Himself to him with a form *(bi al-tajallî al-sûrî)*, this type of manifestation is known among the masters of spiritual states and stations *(arbâb al-hâl wa al-maqâm)*, and it consists in being reminded of His qualities *(hay'atihi)* and reflecting upon His vision *(ru'yatihi)*, which is the outcome of the perfection of one's self-detachment *(takhliyatihi)* and self-adornment *(tahliyatihi)*. And Allah knows best about the states of His Prophets and Intimate Friends whom He has raised with His most excellent upbringing, and the mirrors of whose hearts He has polished with His most excellent polish, until they witnessed the Station of Divine Presence and Abiding *(maqâm al-hudûr wa al-baqâ')*, and they rid themselves of the rust of screens and extinction *(sada' al-huzûr wa al-fanâ')*. May Allah bestow on us their yearnings, may He make us taste their states and manners, and may He make us die in the condition of loving them and raise us in their group.[180]

Al-Qari goes on to quote Ibn al-Qayyim's relation from Ibn Taymiyya that when the Prophet ﷺ saw that his Lord put His hand between his shoulders, he honored that place with the extremity of the turban. Elsewhere he states:

---

[179] Al-Razi, *Asas al-Taqdis*, as quoted by al-Kawthari in *Daf' Shubah al-Tashbih* (p. 32-33 n.). Cf. al-Bayhaqi, *al-Asma' wa al-Sifat* (p. 300-301).
[180] Al-Qari, *Jam' al-Wasa'il* (p. 209).

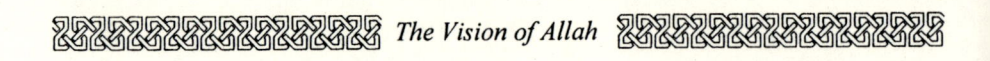

Ibn Sadaqa said that Abu Zur'a said: 'The hadith of Ibn 'Abbas [about the Prophet seeing His Lord] is sound *(sahîh)*, and no one denies it except a *Mu'tazili'*... Ibn al-Humam said: 'This is but the veil of form *(hijâb al-sûra)*.' It seems that he meant by this that the entire goal can be visualized if it is interpreted as a formal manifestation *(tajallî sûrî)*, as it is of necessity absurd to interpret it as a real or literal manifestation *(tajallî haqiqî)*. Allah Almighty has many forms of manifestations *(anwâ' min al-tajalliyât)* according to His Entity and Attributes. Likewise, He possesses all power and encompassing ability, well beyond the angels and other than them, to fashion forms and appearances. Yet He is transcendent above possessing a body *(jism)*, a form *(sûra)*, and directions *(jihât)* with regard to His Entity. These considerations help solve many of the purported difficulties in the ambiguous verses and the narrations of the Attributes. Allah knows best the reality of spiritual stations and the minutiae of objectives.... If the hadith is shown to have something in its chain that indicates forgery, then fine; otherwise: the door of figurative interpretation is wide and imposes itself *(bâb al-ta'wîl wâsi'un muhattam)*.[181]

Elsewhere al-Qari states:

If this vision took place in dream, then there is no difficulty.... However, if it took place in a wakeful state *(fî al-yaqaza)*, as conveyed by the letter of Ahmad ibn Hanbal's narration [but see al-Haytami's comment quoted above], then the *Salaf* declared belief in the letter of such narrations – provided they were sound – without explaining them as one would explain the attributes of creatures. Rather, they negated modality *(al-kayfiyya)* and entrusted knowledge of their hidden meaning to Allah. For He shows to His Prophet ﷺ whatever He wishes from behind the curtains of the Unseen, including what our minds have no way of comprehending. However, to leave aside figurative interpretation *(al-ta'wîl)* in our time fosters confusion *(fitna)* in the beliefs of people, due to the dissemination of the doctrines of misguidance *(i'tiqâdât al-dalâl)*. Therefore, it is appropriate to interpret it in conformity with the Law as a possible intrepretation, not a definitive one. Accordingly, the words 'in the best form' could signify 'I saw my Lord as I was in the

---

[181] Al-Qari, *al-Asrar al-Marfu'a* (2nd ed. p. 209-210 #209; 1st ed. p. 126 #478).

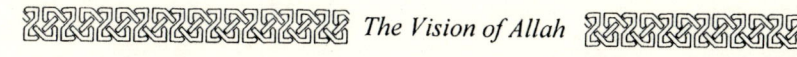

best form in the sense of His utmost favor and kindness to me'; or 'in the Lord's best form' in the sense that the form of something is whatever distinguishes it from something else, whether it pertains to the thing itself or to whatever part of it is being characterized. This can be applied to meanings just as it is applied to material bodies. One speaks about 'picturing a matter or a situation thus.' Allah's 'form' – and Allah knows best – would then be His specific Entity *(dhâtuhu al-makhsûsa)* separate from any other representation of the farthest levels of perfection, or the Attribute that is specific to Him, meaning 'My Lord was more gracious and kinder than at any other time.' Thus did al-Tibi and al-Tawrabashti relate it.[182]

The above is reminiscent of Ibn al-Jawzi's similar interpretation in the second hadith of his *Daf' Shubah al-Tashbih*:

> If we say that he ﷺ saw Him while awake, then the form, if we say that it refers to Allah Almighty, would mean: "I saw Him in the best of His Attributes in turning to me and being pleased with me." If we say that it refers to the Prophet ﷺ himself, then it would mean: "I saw Him as I was in the best form."[183]

Others considered Ibn 'Abbas' narration to refer to a vision with the eyes of the heart, as elucidated by Ibn 'Abbas' other narrations in *Sahih Muslim* and al-Tirmidhi *(hasan)*: "He saw him with his heart." Another narration from Ibn 'Abbas in Muslim states: "He saw him with his heart twice," in commentary of the verses: ❮The heart lied not (in seeing) what it saw❯ (53:11), ❮And verily he saw him, yet another time❯ (53:13).

---

[182] Al-Qari, *al-Mirqat* (1892 ed. 5:303). Al-Mubarakfuri in *Tuhfa al-Ahwadhi* (9:73-74) rejects al-Qari's words "to leave aside figurative interpretation in our time fosters confusion due to the dissemination of the doctrines of misguidance" on the grounds that they contravene – in his view – the method of the *Salaf*, a proof of al-Mubarakfuri's leaning towards unenlightened literalism. Al-Shatibi said in *al-Muwafaqat* (2:332): "The Congregation of [Sunni] Muslims follow Imam Malik's position [in the detestation of *kalâm*], except if one is obliged to speak. One must not remain silent if his purpose is to refute falsehood and guide people away from it, or if one fears the spread of misguidance or some similar danger."

[183] Ibn al-Jawzi, *Daf' Shubah al-Tashbih* (Kawthari ed. p. 32).

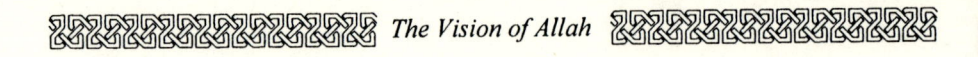

Another explanation is that the Prophet ﷺ saw light. This is stated explicitly in the Prophet's ﷺ reply, when asked by Abu Dharr if he had actually seen his Lord: "I saw light."[184]

Many sound reports show that the Companions differed sharply whether the Prophet ﷺ saw Allah or not. Ibn 'Abbas related that he did, while Ibn Mas'ud, 'A'isha, Abu Hurayra, and Abu Dharr related reports to the contrary, stating that the verses of Sura al-Najm and other Suras referred to Jibril, and that the Prophet ﷺ said that he saw light.

Al-Bukhari narrated from Masruq that the latter said:

I said to 'A'isha: "O my mother! Did Muhammad ﷺ see his Lord?" She replied: "My hair stands on end because of what you said. Have you no idea of three things — whoever tells them to you is lying? [First,] whoever tells you that Muhammad ﷺ saw his Lord, is lying." She then recited: ⟨**Vision comprehends Him not, but He comprehends (all) vision. He is the Subtle, the Aware.**⟩ (6:103) ⟨**And it was not (vouchsafed) to any mortal that Allah should speak to him unless (it be) by revelation or from behind a veil**⟩ (42:51). "[Second,] whoever tells you that he knows what shall happen tomorrow, is lying." She then recited: ⟨**No soul knoweth what it will earn tomorrow**⟩ (31:34). "And [third,] whoever tells you that he concealed something, is lying." She then recited: ⟨**O Messenger! Make known that which has been revealed unto you from your Lord, for if you do it not, you will not have conveyed His message. Allah will protect you from mankind. Lo! Allah guides not the disbelieving folk.**⟩ (5:67) "However, he did see Jibril عليه السلام in his actual form twice."

This hadith is also narrated from Masruq by Muslim thus:

I was sitting back in 'A'isha's house when she said: "O Abu 'A'isha [i.e. Masruq], there are three things, whoever says any of which, he is lying about Allah in the most hateful manner." I asked: "Which things?" She said: "[First,] whoever tells you that Muhammad ﷺ saw his Lord, he is lying about Allah in the most hateful manner." I was sitting back, so I sat up and said: "O Mother of the Believers! Give

---

[184]Narrated by Muslim, al-Tirmidhi *(hasan)*, and Ahmad through four chains.

me a moment and do not rush me. Did not Allah Almighty say: ❨**Surely he beheld him on the clear horizon**❩ (81:23), ❨**And verily he saw him, yet another time**❩ (53:13)?" She replied: "I am the first in this entire Community to have asked Allah's Messenger ﷺ about this, and he said: 'It is but Jibril, I did not see him in the actual form in which he was created other than these two times. I saw him alighting from the heaven, covering it all. The magnitude of his frame spans what lies between the heaven and the earth.'" Then she said: "Did you not hear Allah say: ❨**Vision comprehends Him not, but He comprehends (all) vision. He is the Subtle, the Aware**❩ (6:103)? Did you not hear Allah say: ❨**And it was not (vouchsafed) to any mortal that Allah should speak to him unless (it be) by revelation or from behind a veil, or (that) He sends a messenger to reveal what He will by His leave. Lo! He is Exalted, Wise**❩ (42:51)?" She continued: "[Second,] whoever claims that Allah's Messenger ﷺ concealed any part of Allah's Book, he is lying about Allah in the most hateful manner when Allah is saying: ❨**O Messenger! Make known that which has been revealed unto you from your Lord, for if you do it not, you will not have conveyed His message**❩ (5:67)." She continued: "[Third,] whoever claims that he can tell what shall happen tomorrow, he is lying about Allah in the most hateful manner, since Allah is saying: ❨**Say: None in the heavens and the earth knoweth the Unseen save Allah [and they know not when they will be raised again]**❩ (27:65)."[185]

Muslim mentions another wording which adds the phrase:

She said: "If Muhammad ﷺ had concealed anything of what was revealed to him, he would have concealed this verse: ❨**And when you said unto him on whom Allah has conferred favor and you have conferred favor: Keep your wife to yourself, and fear Allah. And you did hide in your mind that which Allah was to bring to light, and you did fear mankind whereas Allah had a better right that you should fear Him**❩ (33:37)."

A narration by al-Tirmidhi from al-Sha'bi cites the two positions in context:

---

[185] Also narrated from Masruq by al-Tirmidhi *(hasan sahih)*.

Ibn 'Abbas met Ka'b [al-Ahbar] in 'Arafa and asked him about something, whereupon Ka'b began to shout *Allahu Akbar!* until the mountains answered him. Ibn 'Abbas said: "We are the Banu Hashim!"[186] Ka'b said: "Allah has apportioned His vision and His speech between Muhammad and Musa. Musa spoke with Him twice and Muhammad saw him twice." Masruq said: "Later[187] I went to visit 'A'isha and asked: 'Did Muhammad see his Lord?' She replied: 'You have said something that makes my hair stand on end.' I said: 'Do not rush!' and recited [the verses which conclude with][188] the verse ⟪**Verily he saw one of the greater revelations of his Lord**⟫ (53:18). She said: 'Where is this taking you? It was but Jibril. Whoever tells you that Muhammad saw his Lord, or concealed something which he was commanded [to reveal], or knew the five things which Allah mentioned ⟪**Lo! Allah! With Him is knowledge of the Hour. He sends down the rain [and knows that which is in the wombs. No soul knows what it will earn tomorrow, and no soul knows in what land it will die. Lo! Allah is Knower, Aware]**⟫ (31:34) – he has told an enormous lie. Rather, he saw Jibril, whom he did not see in his actual form except twice: once at the Lote-Tree of the Farthest Boundary *(sidra al-muntaha)*, and once in Jiyâd [in Mecca], with his six hundred wings, he had filled the firmament."

Ibn Hajar analyzed this issue at length in his works[189] and compiled a monograph on the topic titled *al-Ghunya fi al-Ru'ya*. Al-Qari also gave an authoritative discussion of the topic in *al-Mirqat*.[190]

---

[186] Al-Tibi said: "[Ibn 'Abbas said] this in order to urge him to be quiet, stop his irritation, and reflect upon the answer, meaning: 'We are people of science and knowledge, we do not ask about things which should be considered so far-fetched.' Because of this, he reflected and gave him his answer." In al-Mubarakfuri, *Tuhfa al-Ahwadhi* (9:118 #3496).

[187] Al-Tibi said: "It appears from this wording that Masruq was present at the time of the exchange that took place between Ka'b and Ibn 'Abbas." In al-Mubarakfuri, *Tuhfa al-Ahwadhi* (9: 119).

[188] This gloss is by al-Tibi, who said: "It is confirmed by al-Tirmidhi's other narration stating: 'O Mother of the Believers! Give me a moment and do not rush me. Did not Allah Almighty say: ⟪**And verily he saw him, yet another time**⟫ (53:13), ⟪**Surely he beheld him on the clear horizon**⟫ (81:23)?'" Al-Mubarakfuri confirmed al-Tibi's reading. In *Tuhfa al-Ahwadhi* (9: 119).

[189] Cf. *Fath al-Bari* (1959 ed. 1:125-135 #50, 8:608-610, 11:463-469 #6204) and *al-Isaba* (2:405-406).

[190] *Al-Mirqat* (1892 ed. 5:306f.).

Appendix 4

Allah's "Hand"[192]

Ibn Wahb: "I heard Malik [ibn Anas] say: 'Whoever recites ❪Allah's Hand❫ (3:73, 5:64, 48:10, 57:29) and indicates his hand, or recites ❪Allah's Eye❫ (cf. 20:39, 11:37, 23:27, 52:48, 54:14) and indicates that organ of his: let it be cut off to discipline him over Allah's sacredness and transcendence above what he has compared Him to, and above his own comparison to Him. Both his life and the limb he compared to Allah are cut off.'"[193]

Ibn 'Asakir wrote:

The *Mu'tazila* said: He has a "hand" *(yad)* but His "hand" is his power *(qudra)* and favor *(ni'ma)*, while His "face" *(wajh)* is His existence. The *Hashwiyya* said: His hand is a limb *(jâriha)*, and His face has a form *(sûra)*.[194] Al-Ash'ari took the middle road and said: His hand is an attribute and His face is an attribute, just like His hearing and His sight.[195]

The *Salaf* and later scholars interpreted Allah's Hand in various ways. Concerning the verse ❪We have built the heaven with (Our) hands❫ (51:47), al-Tabari narrated in his *Tafsir* that Ibn 'Abbas said: "It means: with strength." He reports an identical position from Mujahid, Qatada, Mansur, Ibn Zayd, and Sufyan al-Thawri. This is also Imam al-Ash'ari's explanation a reported by Ibn Furak in the latter's recension of Ash'ari's school.[196] However, al-Ash'ari in *al-Ibana* and his student Ibn Khafif pointed out the difference between the plural hands *(aydin)* on the one hand, and the singular and dual on the other.[197] The *ta'wîl* of the *Salaf* with regard to the plural

---

[192] Also see above, section entitled "Allah's Hand, Palm, Fingers, etc." (p. 36).
[193] In Ibn al-'Arabi al-Maliki, *Ahkam al-Qur'an* (4:1740).
[194] This is the "Salafi" position as stated by 'Abd Allah al-Hashidi in his comments on al-Bayhaqi's *al-Asma' wa al-Sifat*: see above, n. 75.
[195] Ibn 'Asakir, *Tabyin Kadhib al-Muftari* (p. 150-151).
[196] Abu Bakr ibn Furak, *Mujarrad Maqalat al-Ash'ari* (Beirut, 1987) p. 44.
[197] Ibn Khafif said: "Allah created Adam with His Hand – not 'the Hand that is His Power' but 'the Hand that is His Attribute.'" This is to preclude the negation of the attribute of Hand which the *Mu'tazila* practiced, hence al-Ash'ari's statement in the

hands is based on the lexical possibility of the meaning of *al-yad* among the Arabs as signifiying strength *(al-quwwa)*. Thus the same verse (51:47) is cited in al-Zabidi's massive Arabic dictionary as an illustration that "hands" means "strength."[197] This is also the interpretation retained by al-Nawawi in his commentary on Muslim's *Sahih* and other later Ash'aris. It is confirmed by the verse: ⟪**Make mention of our bondmen, Abraham, Isaac and Jacob, men of parts** [literally "of two hands"] **and vision**⟫ (38:45) meaning men possessing strength. It also means ownership *(al-mulk)* as He said: ⟪**Lo! the bounty is in Allah's hand**⟫ (3:73). According to some scholars it also means favor *(al-ni'ma)*, as it is said: "So-and-so has a hand over so-and-so," to mean that he owes him a favor. It also means a kind of link, as Allah said: ⟪**Or he agrees to forego it in whose hand is the marriage tie**⟫ (2:237).

These interpretations are all acceptable and they do not imply the slightest denial of any of Allah's Attributes on which there is consensus. We should nevertheless obligatorily believe that the word *yad* (hand) does not mean an organ as we know it, in accordance with the verse: ⟪**There is nothing whatsoever like unto Him**⟫ (42:11) and that the word *yad* does not imply a resemblance to creatures. Hence Ibn Hajar's statement: "The elite of the *mutakallimûn* said: 'He knows not Allah, who attributes Him resemblance to His creation, or attributes a hand to Him, or a son.'"[198] Contrary to this the doctrine of the Literalists consists in attributing an actual hand to the Creator. Thus Bin Baz charges al-Qadi 'Iyad and Ibn Hajar with abandoning the way of *Ahl al-Sunna* for stating that Allah's Hand does not pertain to a bodily appendage.[199] This is similar to the pretext of the anthropomorphist who said: "We expelled Ibn Hibban from Sijistan for his lack of Religion: he used to say that Allah is not limited."[200]

Ibana (Sabbagh ed. p. 101; 'Uyun ed. p. 108): "The interpretation of ⟪**both My Hands**⟫ as "My Power" [in the verse ⟪**that which I have created with both My hands**⟫ (38:75)] is false in many ways." However, the interpretation of Allah's Hands to signify power or strength is used in the Ash'ari school according to Arabic usage, while asserting Allah's Attribute of Hand. In the verses ⟪**Among the things which Our Hands have fashioned**⟫ (36:71); ⟪**We have built the heaven with Hands**⟫ (51:47), "Hands" signifies strength as in *Lisan al-'Arab, Mukhtar al-Sihah, Mufradat Alfaz al-Qur'an*, and *al-Nihaya*. See Appendix 4, "Allah's 'Hand'" (p. 81).
[197]*Taj al-'Arus* (10:417).
[198]Ibn Hajar, *Fath al-Bari* (1959 ed. 3:361 #1425).
[199]Ibn Hajar, *Fath al-Bari* (1959 ed. 3:361 n.; 1989 ed. 3:357 n.).
[200]See Ibn al-Subki, *Tabaqat al-Shafi'iyya al-Kubra* (3:132) and his stand-alone, edited *Qa'ida fi al-jarh wa al-Ta'dil* (p. 31-33) [*Tabaqat al-Shafi'iyya al-Kubra* (3:13)].

Allah's "Hand"

As for the saying reported from the Prophet ﷺ: "The Black Stone is Allah's right hand,"[202] if established as true, then it is interpreted figuratively according to the doctrinal necessity that Allah is neither spatially confined anywhere nor divisible, and the fact that the senses witness that the Black Stone is not really the right hand of Allah. Therefore, the hadith is taken variously to mean prosperity, blessing, acceptance, and the context of the Muslims pledge of loyalty to their Creator. Yet Ibn Rajab relates that Ibn al-Fa'us al-Hanbali (d. 521) would say: "The Black Stone is Allah's Right Hand in reality *(haqîqatan),*" for which he was nicknamed "The Stony" *(al-Hajarî).*[203] Ibn Furak writes that he embarked on a study of *kalâm* because of this hadith.[204] Ibn Qutayba said that it was actually a saying of Ibn 'Abbas, and he relates a saying of 'A'isha that the Black Stone is the depository of the covenant of human souls with Allah on the Day of Promise *(alastu bi rabbikum).*[205] Ibn Hajar cites al-Khattabi's and al-Muhibb al-Tabari's interpretations of the Black Stone as representing the place where one declares one's pledge of fidelity to the Sovereign.[206]

Another hadith brought up by the anthropomorphists is the narration of Abu Hurayra with a sound chain in Muslim and Ibn Hibban's *Sahih*s that "The Prophet ﷺ recited the verse ⁅**Lo! Allah commands you that you restore deposits to their owners, and, if you judge between mankind, that you judge justly. Lo! excellent is this which Allah admonishes you. Lo! Allah is ever Hearer, Seer**⁆ (4:58) whereupon he ﷺ placed his thumb on his ear and his index finger on his eye." This hadith must be read together with Ibn Hibban's commentary:

---

[202] Narrated from Ibn 'Abbas, Jabir, Anas, and others by Ibn Abi 'Umar al-Ma'dani in his *Musnad,* al-Tabarani, al-Suyuti in his *Jami' al-saghir* (1:516 #3804-3805), Ibn 'Asakir in *Tarikh Dimashq* (15:90-92), and others. It is considered *da'if* (weak) by Ibn al-Jawzi, Ibn 'Adi, and Albani, while others consider it forged. Cf. al-Ahdab, *Zawa'id Tarikh Baghdad* (5:321-323 #949). However, al-'Ajluni stated that it is *sahîh* as a halted report from Ibn 'Abbas as narrated by al-Quda'i in the wording: "The Corner [of the Black Stone] *(al-rukn)* is Allah's Right Hand on earth...," and declared it *hasan* as a hadith of the Prophet ﷺ. Its mention in the *Reliance of the Traveller* (p. 853b) as "narrated by al-Hakim, who declared it *sahîh*, from 'Abd Allah ibn 'Amr," is incorrect.
[203] Ibn Rajab, *Dhayl Tabaqat al-Hanabila* (1:173-174 #74).
[204] As related by Ibn al-Subki in *Tabaqat al-Shafi'iyya* (4:129).
[205] Ibn Qutayba, *Ta'wil Mukhtalaf al-hadith* (p. 215).
[206] In *Fath al-Bari* (1959 ed. 3:463 #1520).

◇◇◇◇◇◇◇◇◇ *Allah's "Hand"* ◇◇◇◇◇◇◇◇◇

By placing his fingers on his ear and eye the Prophet ﷺ wanted to let people know that Allah Almighty does not hear by means of the ear that has an auditory meatus and curves, nor does He see with the eye that has eyelids, a pupil, and a white part. Highly exalted is our Lord above any likeness with His creatures in any way whatsoever! Rather, He hears and sees without organ *(âla)* in any way He wishes.[206]

Ibn 'Abd al-Salam gave the following *fatwa* concerning the interpretation of *yad*:

Q. What is the meaning of the Prophet's ﷺ saying: "The heart of the believer is between two fingers of the Merciful, He turns it over as He wishes"?[207] Does one contravene his obligation if he says: "I do not say anything concerning the verses and the hadiths on the attributes. Rather I hold the same belief concerning them as the Pious Salaf held. To speak about them is an innovation *(bid'a)*, and I let them pass according to their external sense," or is interpretation necessary?

A. The meaning of the Prophet's ﷺ saying, "The heart of the believer is between two fingers of the Merciful" is that Allah exerts His custody over it with His power and determination as He wills, changing it from disbelief to belief and from obedience to disobedience or the reverse.

It is like His saying: ❲**Blessed is He in Whose hand is the dominion**❳ (67:1) and: ❲**O Prophet! Say unto those captives who are in your hands**❳ (8:70). It is understood that the captives were not left in the physical hands of the Muslims but that they were subdued and conquered by them. The same applies to the expressions: "Specific and non-specific matters are in the hand of so-and-so," and "The slaves and the animals are in the hand of so-and-so." It is

---

[206] Ibn Hibban, *Sahih* (1:498 #265).
[207] Narrated from 'Abd Allah ibn 'Amr by Muslim and from al-Nawwas ibn Sam'an by Ahmad, al-Nasa'i, Ibn Majah, Ibn Hibban in his *Sahih*, al-Hakim, and others, all with sound chains. Al-Hakim declared the hadith sound and al-Dhahabi concurred. The continuation of the hadith states that the Prophet ﷺ used to say: "O Transformer of hearts! Make firm our hearts in Your Religion," and that he also said: "And the balance is in the Merciful's hand, He elevates a people while he abases others, and so until the Day of Resurrection."

understood that all these mean that they are in his control *(istîlâ')* and disposal and not in his physical hand. Similarly Allah's saying: ⟨**Or he agrees to forgo it in whose hand is the marriage tie**⟩ (2:237). The marriage tie is not in his physical hand, but the hand is only an expression of his empowerment and his ability to dispose of the matter.

For one to say: "I believe in this matter what the *Salaf* believed" is a lie. How does he believe what he has no idea about, and the meaning of which he does not know?

Nor is speaking about the meaning a reprehensible innovation, but rather an obligatory excellent innovation *(bid'a hasana wâjiba)*, whenever something dubious appears. The only reason the *Salaf* kept away from such discourse is that in their time no-one construed the words of Allah and those of His Prophet to mean what it is not permissible to construe them to mean. If any such dubiousness had appeared in their time they would have shown it to be a lie and rejected it strenuously! Thus did the Companions and the Salaf refute the *Qadariyya* when the latter brought out their innovation, although they did not use to address such matters before the *Qadariyya* appeared on the scene. Nor did they reply to the individuals who mentioned them. Nor did any of the Companions relate any of it from the Prophet ﷺ since there was no need for it. And Allah knows best."[209]

---

[209] Al-'Izz ibn 'Abd al-Salam, *Fatawa* (p. 55-57).

Appendix 5

Istiwâ' Is A Divine Act

Imam Abu al-Hasan al-Ash'ari said: "Allah's establishment on the Throne is an action He has created named *istiwâ'* and related to the Throne, just as He has created an action named *ityân* (coming) related to a certain people; and this implies neither descent nor movement."[210] Al-Bayhaqi confirmed this: "Abu al-Hasan 'Ali al-Ash'ari said that Allah Almighty effected an act in relation to the Throne, and He called that act *istiwâ'*, just as He effected other acts in relation to other objects, and He called those acts 'sustenance' *(rizq)*, 'favor' *(ni'ma)*, or other of His acts."[211] This is also the interpretation of Ibn Hazm (d. 456) – although a vehement enemy of Ash'aris – who explains *istiwâ'* as "an act pertaining to the Throne".[212]

Abu al-Fadl al-Tamimi mentioned that two positions were reported from Imam Ahmad concerning *istiwâ'*: One group narrated that he considered it "of the attributes of action" *(min sifât al-fi'l)*, another, "of the attributes of the Entity" *(min sifât al-dhât)*."[213] Ibn Battal mentions that *Ahl al-Sunna* hold either one of these two positions: "Those that interpreted *istawâ* as 'He exalted Himself' consider *istiwâ* an attribute of the Entity, while those who interpreted it otherwise consider it an attribute of action."[214]

Al-Tamimi further related that Ahmad said:

> [*Istiwâ'*]: It means height/exaltation *('uluw)* and elevation *(irtifâ')*. Allah is ever exalted *('âlî)* and elevated *(rafî')* without beginning, before He created the Throne. He is above everything *(huwa fawqa kulli shay')*, and He is exalted over everything *(huwa al-'âlî 'alâ kulli shay')*. He only specified the Throne because of its particular significance which makes it different from everything else, as the Throne is the best of all things and the most elevated of them.

---

[210] As cited in 'Abd al-Qahir al-Baghdadi, *Usul al-Din* (p. 113).
[211] Al-Bayhaqi, *al-Asma' wa al-Sifat* (2:308).
[212] In his *al-Fisal fi al-Milal* (2:125).
[213] Ibn Abi Ya'la, *Tabaqat al-Hanabila* (2:296).
[214] In Ibn Hajar, *Fath al-Bari* (1959 ed. 13:409).

Istiwâ' Is A Divine Act

Allah therefore praised Himself by saying that He ⟪established Himself over the Throne⟫, that is, He exalted Himself over it *('alayhi 'alâ)*. It is impermissible to say that He established Himself with a contact or a meeting with it. Exalted is Allah above that! Allah is not subject to change, substitution, nor limits, whether before or after the creation of the Throne.[214]

The Maliki scholar Ibn Abi Jamra (d. 695) said something similar in his commentary on the hadith "Allah wrote a Book before He created creation, saying: Verily My mercy precedeth My wrath; and it is written with Him above the Throne":

> It may be said from the fact that the Book is mentioned as being "above the Throne" that the divine wisdom has decreed for the Throne to carry whatever Allah wishes of the record of His judgment, power, and the absolute unseen known of Him alone, in order to signify the exclusivity of His encompassing knowledge regarding these matters. This makes the Throne one of the greatest signs of the exclusivity of His knowledge of the Unseen. This could explain the verse of *istiwâ'* as referring to whatever Allah wills of His power, which is the Book He has placed above His Throne."[215]

Sufyan al-Thawri (d. 161) interpreted *istiwâ'* in the verse ⟪Allah established Himself over the Throne⟫ (20:4) as "a command concerning the Throne" *(amrun fi al-'arsh)*, as related by Imam al-Haramayn al-Juwayni (d. 478) in *al-Irshad* and quoted by al-Yafi'i in the latter's book Kitab *Marham al-'Ilal al-Mu'dila fi Daf' al-Shubah wa al-Radd 'ala al-Mu'tazila* ("Book of the Resolution of Difficult Problems for the Removal of Doubts and the Refutation of the Mu'tazila"):

> The understanding of *istiwâ'* as Allah's turning to a particular command concerning the Throne is not far-fetched, and this is the *ta'wîl* of Imam Sufyan al-Thawri, who took as corroborating evidence for it the verse: ⟪Then turned He *(thumma istawâ)* to the heaven when it was smoke⟫ (41:11).[216]

---

[214] Ibn Abi Ya'la, *Tabaqat al-Hanabila* (2:296-297).
[215] Ibn Hajar, *Fath al-Bari, Tawhid* ch. 22 (1959 ed. 13:414; 1989 ed. 13:508 #7422).
[216] In al-Yafi'i, *Marham al-'Ilal* (p. 245).

Istiwâ' Is A Divine Act

Al-Tabari said, in his commentary on the verse ⟪**Then turned He** *(thumma istawâ)* **to the heaven, and fashioned it as seven heavens**⟫ (2:29):

> The meaning of *istiwâ'* in this verse is height *('uluw)* and elevation... but if one claims that this means displacement for Allah, tell him: He is high and elevated over the heaven with the height of sovereignty and power, not the height of displacement and movement to and fro.

The above position is exactly that of the Ash'ari school, as shown by Abu Bakr ibn al-'Arabi's and Ibn Hajar's numerous comments to that effect[218] directed against those who attribute altitude to Allah in their conception of His *'uluw* such as Ibn Taymiyya. The latter stated: "The Creator, Glorified and Exalted is He, is above the world and His being above is literal, not in the sense of dignity or rank."[219] This doctrine was comprehensively refuted by Ibn Jahbal al-Kilabi (d. 733) in his *Radd Madhhab Ibn Taymiyya fi Ithbat al-Jiha* ("The Refutation of Ibn Taymiyya's Doctrine Which Attributes a Direction to Allah").[220]

Ibn al-Jawzi (d. 597) in the introduction of his *Daf' Shubah al-Tashbih* said of the anthropomorphists: "They are not content to say: 'attribute of action' *(sifatu fi'l)* until they end up saying: 'attribute of the Essence' *(sifatu dhât)*." Ibn Hazm also said: "If the establishment on the Throne is eternal without beginning, then the Throne is eternal without beginning, and this is disbelief."[221]

Al-Bayhaqi quotes one of the companions of al-Ash'ari, Abu al-Hasan 'Ali ibn Muhammad ibn Mahdi al-Tabari (d. ~380) as saying in his book *Ta'wil al-Ahadith al-Mushkilat al-Waridat fi al-Sifat* ("Interpretation of the Problematic Narrations That Pertain to the Attributes"): "Allah is in the heaven above everything and established over His Throne in the sense that He is exalted *('âlin)* above it, and the sense of *istiwâ'* is self-elevation

---

[218] Respectively in *'Arida al-Ahwadhi* (2:234-237) and *Fath al-Bari* (3:37-38, 6:136 [*Jihad*], also *Tawhid* ch. 23 last par.).
[219] In *al-Ta'sis al-Radd 'ala Asas al-Taqdis* (1:111).
[220] Its text is reproduced in Ibn al-Subki's *Tabaqat* (9:35-91) and translated in full in a separate publication.
[221] In *al-Fisal* (2:124). See also above, al-Bayhaqi's explanation in *al-Asma' wa al-Sifat*, section entitled "Allah's Establishment over the Throne" (p. 42).

(i'tilâ')."²²¹ This is the most widespread interpretation *(ta'wîl)* of the issue among the *Salaf*: al-Baghawi said that the meaning of the verse ⟨**The Merciful established Himself over the Throne**⟩ (20:5) according to Ibn 'Abbas and most of the commentators of Qur'an is "He elevated Himself" *(irtafa'a)*.²²² This is the interpretation quoted by Bukhari in his *Sahih* from the senior *Tâbi'i* Rufay' ibn Mahran Abu al-'Aliya (d. 90). Bukhari also cites from Mujahid (d. 102) the interpretation "to rise above" or "exalt Himself above" *('alâ)*. Ibn Battal declares the latter to be the true position and the saying of Ahl al-Sunna because Allah described Himself as ***al-'Alî*** (2:255) and said: ⟨**exalted be He** *(ta'âlâ)* **over all that they ascribe as partners (unto Him)!**⟩ (23:92).²²³

In complete opposition to the above Ibn Taymiyya said in his *Fatawa*: "Allah's establishment over the throne is real, and the servant's establishment over the ship is real" *(lillâhi ta'âlâ istiwâ'un 'alâ 'arshihi haqîqatan wa li al-'abdi istiwâ'un 'alâ al-fulki haqîqatan)*.²²⁴ "Allah is with us in reality, and He is above His throne in reality *(Allâhu ma'ana haqîqatan wa huwa fawqa al-'arshi haqîqatan)*.... Allah is with His creation in reality and He is above His Throne in reality *(Allahu ma'a khalqihi haqîqatan wa huwa fawqa al-'arshi haqîqatan)*."²²⁵

Another interpretation commonly used by some Ash'aris for *istiwâ'* is that of *istîlâ'* and *qahr*, respectively "establishing sovereignty" and "subduing." Ibn Battal and Abu Mansur al-Baghdadi attribute this interpretation chiefly to the *Mu'tazila*. Ibn Hajar said:

> The *Mu'tazila* said its meaning is "establishing sovereignty through subjugation and overpowering" *(al-istîlâ' bi al-qahr wa al-ghalaba)*, citing as a proof the saying of the poet:
>
> > *qad istawâ Bishrun 'ala al-'Irâq*
> > *min ghayri sayfin wa damin muhrâq*

---

²²¹In al-Bayhaqi, *al-Asma' wa al-Sifat* (2:308).
²²²As reported by Ibn Hajar in *Fath al-Bari* (1959 ed. 13:409), book of *Tawhid*, chapter 22.
²²³Ibn Hajar, *ibid*.
²²⁴Ibn Taymiyya, *Majmu' al-Fatawa*, Vol. 5 entitled *al-Asma' wa al-Sifat* (5:199).
²²⁵*Op. cit.* (5:103).

Bishr established mastery over Iraq
without sword and without shedding blood.

The anthropomorphists *(al-jismiyya)* said: "Its meaning is settledness *(al-istiqrâr)*."²²⁷ Some of *Ahl al-Sunna* said: "Its meaning is He elevated Himself *(irtafa'a)*" while others of them said: "Its meaning is He rose above *('alâ)*," and others of them said: "Its meaning is sovereignty *(al-mulk)* and power *(al-qudra)*."²²⁸

The latter Sunni interpretation is evidently similar to that of *istîlâ'* and *qahr*. However, because the *Mu'tazila* claimed that the divine Attributes were originated in time rather than uncreated and beginningless, their interpretation was rejected by the scholars of *Ahl al-Sunna*. Ibn Battal said: "The *Mu'tazila* position is null and void, for Allah is *qâhir*, *ghâlib*, and *mustawlî* without beginning."²²⁹ Ibn Battal is referring to the Ash'ari position whereby the Attributes of acts such as creation, although connected with created objects, are without beginning in relation to Allah.²³⁰ To those who object to *istawlâ*

---

²²⁷The explanation of *istawâ* as *istaqarra* in the verse ❨Then He established Himself over the Throne❩ (32:4) is actually reported from al-Kalbi and Muqatil by al-Baghawi – in his commentary entitled *Ma'alim al-Tanzil* (al-Manar ed. 3:488) – who adds that the philologist Abu 'Ubayda [Ma'mar ibn al-Muthanna al-Taymi (d. ~210)] said "He mounted" *(sa'ida)*. Pickthall followed the latter in his translation of the verse as ❨Then He mounted the Throne❩. It is a foundational position of the "Salafis" as stated by Imam Muhammad Abu Zahra: "The 'Salafis' and Ibn Taymiyya assert that settledness takes place over the Throne…. Ibn Taymiyya strenuously asserts that Allah descends, and can be above *(fawq)* and below *(taht)* 'without how,' and that the school of the *Salaf* is the affirmation of everything that the Qur'an stated concerning aboveness *(fawqiyya)*, belowness *(tahtiyya)*, and establishment over the Throne." Abu Zahra, *al-Madhahib al-Islamiyya* (p. 320-322).
²²⁸Ibn Hajar, *Fath al-Bari* (1959 ed. 13:409).
²²⁹In *Fath al-Bari* (1959 ed. 13:409).
²³⁰Cf. Abu Nu'aym al-Asbahani in his book *al-I'tiqad* as quoted by al-Dhahabi in *Mukhtasar al-'Uluw* (p. 261 #316): "Our way is the way of the *Salaf* who followed the Book, the Sunna, and the Consensus of the Community. Part of their belief was that Allah is perfect from preternity with all His beginningless Attributes, neither passing away nor changing. He has always been and continues to be *(lam yazal)* [characterized as the] Knower *('âlim)* by [the attribute of] knowledge, [the] Seer *(basîr)* by [the attribute of] sight, [the] Hearer *(samî')* by [the attribute of] hearing, and [the] Speaker *(mutakallim)* by [the attribute of] speech." Later scholars specified that the attributes of act have two types of connection *(ta'alluq)* to the act: "beginninglessly potential" *(salûhî qadîm)* and "actualized in time" *(tanjîzî hâdith)*.

on the grounds that it necessarily supposed prior opposition,²³⁰ Ibn Hajar similarly remarked that that assumption is discarded by the verse: ⟨**Allah was (kâna) ever Knower, Wise**⟩ (4:17), which the scholars explained to mean "He is ever Knower and Wise."²³¹

Thus Dawud al-Zahiri's objection that *istîlâ'* necessitates a wresting from an adversary²³² is not absolute among *Ahl al-Sunna*. The Ash'ari grammarian al-Raghib al-Asfahani (d. 402) said that *istawâ 'alâ* has the meaning of *istawlâ 'alâ* ("He overcame") and cited the verse of *istiwâ* (20:4) as an example of this meaning: "It means that everything is alike in relation to him in such manner that no one thing is nearer to Him than another thing, since He is not like the bodies that abide in one place exclusively of another place."²³³ In this sense, both the *Mu'tazili* position of origination for the Attributes and the literalist requirement of conquest-after-struggle are dismissed, and *istawlâ* can be safely admitted among the interpretations of *Ahl al-Sunna*. As Ibn Battal alluded, "establishing dominion and sovereignty," "subduing," and "conquering" no more suppose prior opposition in the face of the Creator than do His attributes of "All-Victorious" *(Zâhir)* "All-Conquering" *(Qahhâr)*, "Prevailer" *(Ghâlib)*, or "Omnipotent" *(Qâhir)* presuppose resistance or power on anyone's part. This is confirmed by the verses: ⟨**He is the Omnipotent** *(qâhir)* **over His slaves**⟩ (6:18, 6:61) and ⟨**Allah prevails** *(ghâlib)* **in His purpose**⟩ (12:21). Al-Raghib said: "It means that everything is alike in relation to him" and he did not say: "became alike."

Ibn al-Jawzi mentions another reason for permitting this interpretation: "Whoever interprets **and He is with you** (57:4) as meaning 'He is with you in knowledge,' permits his opponent to interpret *istiwâ'* as 'subduing' *(al-qahr)*."²³⁴

As for the linguistic precedent of the meaning *istawlâ* for *istawâ*, it is provided by the poet al-Akhtal (d. <110) who said: "Bishr established

---

²³⁰Cf. Ibn al-A'rabi in al-Dhahabi's *Mukhtasar al-'Uluw* (p. 195 #241) and Dawud al-Zahiri – both of whom are quoted by Ibn Hajar in his discussion in *Fath al-Bari* – and Ibn 'Abd al-Barr in his discussion of the hadith of descent in *al-Tamhid*: "The meaning of *istawlâ* in the language is 'to overcome,' and Allah Almighty does not need to overcome anyone."
²³¹In *Fath al-Bari* (1959 ed. 13:409).
²³²In *Fath al-Bari* (1959 ed. 13:409).
²³³In al-Zabidi, *Taj al-'Arus*, entry s-w-y.
²³⁴In *Daf' Shubah al-Tashbih* (1998 Kawthari repr. p. 23).

mastery over *(istawâ 'alâ)* Iraq without sword and without shedding blood." Some "Salafis" reject this linguistic proof on the ground that al-Akhtal was a second-century Christian. This shows ignorance of agreed-upon criteria for the probativeness of Arabic poetry in the *Shari'a*, which extends at least to the year 150 and applies regardless of creed.[236]

Dr. Muhammad Sa'id Ramadan al-Buti said:

The consensus in place regarding these texts is the refraining from applying to them any meaning which establishes a sameness or likeness between Allah and His creatures, and the refraining from divesting their established lexical tenor.

The obligatory way to proceed is either to explain these words according to their external meanings which conform with Allah's transcendence above any like or partner, and this includes not explaining them as bodily appendages and other corporeal imagery. Therefore it will be said, for example: He has established Himself over the Throne as He has said, with an establishment which befits His majesty and oneness; and He has a hand as He has said, which befits His divinity and majesty; etc.

Or they can be explained figuratively according to the correct rules of language and in conformity with the customs of speech in their historical context. For example: the establishment is the establishment of dominion *(istîlâ')* and that of authority *(tasallut)*; Allah's hand is His strength in His saying: ❨**Allah's hand is over their hand**❩ (48:10) and His generosity in His saying: ❨**Nay, both His hands are spread wide, and He bestows as He wills**❩ (5:64).[237]

As for the interpretation of *istiwâ'* as sitting *(julûs)*, it is asserted by 'Abd Allah ibn Ahmad ibn Hanbal in his book entitled *Kitab al-Sunna* (p. 5, 71): "Is establishment *(istiwâ')* other than by sitting *(julûs)*?" "Allah sits on the *kursî* and there remains only four spans vacant." Al-Khallal in his own *Kitab al-Sunna* (p. 215-216) states that whoever denies that "Allah sits on the *kursî* and there remains only four spans vacant" is an unbeliever. 'Uthman al-Darimi went so far as to say in his *Naqd al-Jahmiyya* (p. 75): "If He so

---

[236] See on this topic 'A'isha al-Hadithiyya, *Hujjiyya al-Sunna*.
[237] Al-Buti, *al-Salafiyya* (p. 132-133).

Istiwā' Is A Divine Act

willed, He could have settled on the back of a gnat and it would have carried Him thanks to His power and the favor of His lordship, not to mention the magnificient Throne." Ibn Taymiyya and Ibn al-Qayyim endorsed these views.[237] Al-Kawthari wrote in his *Maqalat* (p. 358): "Whoever imagines that our Lord sits on the *kursî* and leaves space at His side for His Prophet to sit, he has followed the Christians who believe that 'Isa ﷺ was raised to heaven and sat next to his Father – Allah is elevated above the partnership they ascribe to Him!"

---

[237]Cf. the latter's *Bada'i' al-Fawa'id* (1900 ed. 4:39-40, 1994 ed. 2:328-329).

Appendix 6

Allah's "Coming" And "Arrival"

The mention of Allah's "coming" *(ityân)* and "arrival" *(majî')* in different verses has been interpreted variously by the *Salaf* and later scholars.

Concerning the verses ❴Wait they for naught else than that Allah should come unto them in the shadows of the clouds with the angels?❵ (2:210) and ❴Your Lord shall arrive with angels, rank on rank❵ (89:22):

- The Tabi'i Abu al-'Aliya (d. 90) and al-Rabi' (d. 139) said of the first verse: "It means the angels come in the clouds. It is confirmed by His saying: **'A day when the heaven with the clouds will be rent asunder and the angels will be sent down, a great descent.'** (25:25)"[239]

- Al-Bayhaqi said: "[Abu al-'Aliya's] commentary rightly establishes that the clouds are a place and vehicle only for the angels, whereas there is neither place nor vehicle for Allah Almighty."[240]

- Al-Ash'ari said that Allah Almighty on the Day of Judgment shall bring about a certain act *(fi'l)* which He named "coming" and "arrival."[241]

- Al-Qurtubi reiterated al-Ash'ari's explanation and said: "It is based on the lexical meaning of *ityân*, which is to proceed to do something *(al-qasd ila al-shay')*. The meaning of the verse is thus: Wait they for naught else than that Allah should cause to pass a certain act with some of His creatures whereby He shall proceed to requite them and judge them, just as He brought to be a certain act which He called 'descent' and another which He called 'establishment.'"[242]

---

[239] See n. 102.
[240] *AS* p. 448; *ASH* 2:370 #943.
[241] Narrated by al-Bayhaqi, *AS* (p. 448); *ASH* (2:371).
[242] Al-Qurtubi, *Tafsir* (verse 2:210).

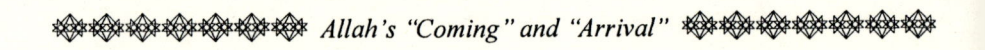

- The grammarian al-Akhfash (d. 210) said that ⟨that Allah should come⟩ (2:210) is not understood literally concerning Allah, but means that His order *(amr)* should come.²⁴²

- The grammarian al-Zajjaj (d. ~310) said: "It means the promised reckoning and punishment shall come to them in the form of a cloud, as in His saying: '**Allah visited them from a place whereof they recked not**' (59:2), that is: by abasing them."²⁴³

- Imam Ahmad likewise interpreted ⟨that Allah should come⟩ (2:210) to mean that His order *(amr)* should come, in the light of His saying: '**Await they aught save that the angels should come unto them or thy Lord's command should come to pass?**' (16:33).²⁴⁴

- Imam Ahmad further interpreted ⟨Your Lord shall arrive⟩ (89:22) to mean His reward *(thawâb)* should come.²⁴⁵ The above reports suffice to refute any claim of a supposed consensus of the *Salaf* whereby they did not interpret Allah's coming as His order.²⁴⁶

- Al-Fakhr al-Razi reiterated Ahmad's interpretation of verse 2:210: "It means that His order should come unto them, as proved by His saying: '**Await they aught save that the angels should come unto them or thy Lord's command should come to pass?**' (16:33). The two verses relate a single event, and one explains the other."²⁴⁷

---

²⁴²As cited by al-Qurtubi in his *Tafsir* (verse 2:210).
²⁴³*Ibid.*
²⁴⁴Narrated by Ibn Hazm in *al-Fisal* (2:173). al-Kawthari in his edition of Bayhaqi's *al-Asma' wa al-Sifat* (p. 448) states that Abu Ya'la also narrates it from Ahmad. See also Ibn al-Jawzi's *Daf' shubah al-tashbih* (p. 110 and 141).
²⁴⁵Narrated through al-Bayhaqi by Ibn Kathir in *al-Bidaya wa al-Nihaya* (10:361), by al-Bayhaqi in *Manaqib Ahmad*, and by Ibn al-Jawzi in *Daf' Shubah al-tashbih* p. 13. Al-Kawthari in *al-Asma'* (p. 292) states that Ahmad interpreted it as *amr*, citing Ibn Hazm.
²⁴⁶"To explain these verses as a reference to the coming or arrival of Allah's order is unsound because it contravenes the literal meaning *(zâhir al-lafz)* of the verse and the consensus of the *salaf*, and there is no proof for it." Muhammad ibn Salih al-'Uthaymin, Commentary on Ibn Taymiyya's *'Aqida Wasitiyya* (Cairo: Maktaba al-'Ilm, p. 23).
²⁴⁷As cited by al-Kawthari, *AS* (p. 447).

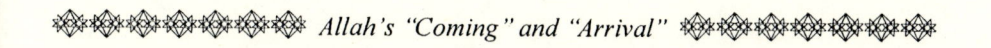

- Al-Razi further said that Allah's saying **'Wait they'** (2:210, 16:33) is referring to the Jews: "His saying: **'O ye who believe! Come, all of you, into submission'** (2:208) was revealed only concerning the Jews.[249] Then His saying **'And if you slide back after the clear proofs have come unto you'** (2:209) addresses the Jews, and therefore His saying **'Wait they'** is referring to them.[250] The meaning is: 'They shall not accept your Religion except if Allah comes to them in the shadows of the clouds so that they can see Him distinctly, for the Jews were anthropomorphists *(mushabbiha)*. They considered it possible for Allah to come and go, and they said that He manifested Himself to Musa on the Mount in the shadows of the clouds. So they asked for something similar in the time of Muhammad, upon him blessings and peace."[251]

---

[249] As established in al-Wahidi's *Asbab al-Nuzul* and Suyuti's *Asbab al-Nuzul*.
[250] This is also the position of Ibn Kathir, al-Qurtubi, and others in the *Tafsir* (verse 2:210).
[251] As cited by al-Kawthari, *AS* (p. 448).

Appendix 7

The Hadith of Allah's "Descent"

The scholars differed concerning the meaning of Allah's "descent" in the mass-narrated *(mutawâtir)* hadith:

> Our Lord – Blessed and Exalted is He! – descends every night to the lowest heaven in the last third of the night and says: Who supplicates Me so that I may answer him? Who asks forgiveness from Me so that I may forgive him?[252]

Ibn 'Asakir said:

> The *Mu'tazila* said: [Allah's] "Descent" *(nuzûl)* is the descent of any given sign of His, or that of His angels. The *Mushabbiha* and *Hashwiyya* said: Descent is the descent of His person *(dhât)* through movement *(haraka)* and displacement *(intiqâl)*. Al-Ash'ari took the middle road and said: Descent is one of His attributes.[253]

Al-Bayhaqi further reports that Al-Ash'ari said: "What is meant by the descent is an act brought to be by Allah in the nearest heaven every night, which [the Prophet ﷺ] has named a descent, without movement nor displacement. Exalted is Allah above the characteristics of creatures!"[254]

Al-Qurtubi said that the hadith is elucidated by that related by al-Nasa'i in his *Sunan al-Kubra* and *'Amal al-Yawm wa al-Layla* whereby the Prophet ﷺ said:

> Allah waits until the first part of the night is over, then He orders a herald *(munâdiyan)* to say: Is there anyone supplicating so that he

---

[252] Narrated from Abu Hurayra by Bukhari, Muslim, Abu Dawud, al-Tirmidhi, Ahmad, Malik, and al-Darimi. It is narrated from twenty-three Companions, as stated by al-Kattani in *Nazm al-Mutanathir*.
[253] Ibn 'Asakir, *Tabyin Kadhib al-Muftari* (p. 151).
[254] As quoted by al-Bayhaqi in *al-Asma' wa al-Sifat* (2:371).

may be answered, anyone begging for forgiveness so that he may be forgiven, any petitioner so that he may be granted his request?²⁵⁴

The above narration is confirmed by the hadith of 'Uthman ibn Abi al-'As al-Thaqafi from the Prophet ﷺ:

> The gates of heaven are opened in the middle of the night and a herald calls out: Is there anyone supplicating so that he may be answered? Is there anyone asking so that he may be granted? Is there anyone afflicted so that he may be delivered? At that time there is no Muslim who invokes for anything except Allah answers him, except an adultress who runs after her pleasure and her intimate companion.²⁵⁵

Thus the calling out, in al-Qurtubi's view, is directly attributed to Allah in Bukhari and Muslim's narrations in order to highlight His regard and His emphasis, as when one says: "The sultan calls out for this," whereas it is actually a herald who calls out the sultan's order as elucidated in the above two versions. It is with respect to the latter that Imam Malik reportedly said: "It is our Blessed and Exalted Lord's order which descends; as for Him, He is eternally the same, He does not move or go to and fro,"²⁵⁶ although it is established that Malik forbade discourse of any kind about the hadiths of Allah's attributes,²⁵⁷ preferring not to interpret the hadiths of descent one way or the other and that he said about them: "Let them pass without entering into modality."²⁵⁸

---

²⁵⁴Narrated from Abu Sa'id al-Khudri and Abu Hurayra by al-Nasa'i in *al-Sunan al-Kubra* (6:124 #10316) and *'Amal al-Yawm wa al-Layla* (p. 340 #482). Al-Qari declared it sound in *Mirqat al-Mafatih* (1994 ed. 3:299).
²⁵⁵Narrated by al-Bazzar, *Kashf al-Astar* (4:44); al-Tabarani, *al-Kabir* (9:51). Al-Haythami declared it sound in *Majma' al-Zawa'id* (10:209). Also narrated – with a weak chain – by Ahmad in his *Musnad*.
²⁵⁶Narrated from Habib ibn Abi Habib by al-Dhahabi in *Syar A'lam al-Nubala'* (8:418), but al-Dhahabi himself reported in *Mizan al-I'tidal* (1:452) that all of Ibn Abi Habib's narrations are forged. Also narrated by Ibn 'Abd al-Barr in *al-Tamhid* (7:143).
²⁵⁷Cf. Ibn Abi Zayd al-Qayrawani, *al-Jami'* p. 124.
²⁵⁸As mentioned by al-Tirmidhi in his *Sunan* (Book of *zakat*, hadith "Verily, Allah accepts the *zakat* and takes it with His right Hand..."), Ibn al-Jawzi in his *Daf' Shubah al-Tashbih* (p. 195-196), al-Dhahabi in *Siyar A'lam al-Nubala* (al-Arna'ut ed. 8:105), and others.

Nevertheless, not all the *Salaf* let them pass, as al-Bayhaqi relates from the Tabi'i Hammad ibn Zayd that he interpreted Allah's descent to the nearest heaven as "His turning to" *(nuzûluhu iqbâluhu)*.[260]

Ibn al-Jawzi cautioned: "Since you understand that the one who descends towards you is near to you, content yourself with the knowledge that He is near you, and do not think in terms of bodily nearness."[261] Ibn al-Jawzi actually read the verb "descend" in the hadith of Bukhari and Muslim as *yunzilu* ("He orders down") instead of *yanzilu* ("He comes down").[262] This was also the Ash'ari imam Ibn Furak's reading according to Ibn Hajar who confirms its soundness, in view of al-Nasa'i's narration. This furthers confirms al-Qurtubi's reading and Hammad ibn Zayd's interpretation.

Ibn Hajar's Commentary

Following is the text of Ibn Hajar's commentary on the hadith of descent:

> Those who assert direction for Allah have used this hadith as proof that He is in the direction of aboveness. The vast majority of the scholars reject this, because such a saying leads to establishing boundaries for Him and Allah is exalted above that.[263]
>
> The meaning of "descent" is interpreted differently:
>
> - Some say that the external meaning is meant literally: these are the *Mushabbiha* and Allah is exalted above what they say.

---

[260] Al-Bayhaqi, *al-Asma' wa al-Sifat* (AS p. 456, ASH 2:380).
[261] Ibn al-Jawzi, *Daf' Shubah al-Tashbih* (p. 196).
[262] *Ibid.* (p. 192).
[263] 'Abd al-'Aziz bin Baz inserted the following footnote at this point: "What he means by 'the vast majority of the scholars' is the vast majority of the scholars of *kalâm*. As for *Ahl al-Sunna* – and these are the Companions and those who followed them in excellence – they assert a direction for Allah, and that is the direction of height, believing that the Exalted is above the Throne without giving an example and without entering into modality. The proofs from the Qur'an and the Sunna for this are innumerable, so take heed and beware. And Allah knows best."

- Some reject the validity of the hadiths cited in that chapter altogether. These are the *Khawârij* and the *Mu'tazila* in their arrogance. What is strange is that they interpret figuratively what is related to this in the Qur'an, but they reject what is in the hadith either out of ignorance or out of obduracy.

- Some have taken them as they have come, believing in them without specificity, declaring Allah to be transcendent above modality *(kayfiyya)* and likeness to creation *(tashbîh)*: these are the vast majority of the *Salaf*. That position is reported by al-Bayhaqi and others from the Four Imams, Sufyan ibn 'Uyayna, Sufyan al-Thawri, Hammad ibn Salama, Hammad ibn Zayd, al-Awza'i, al-Layth, and others.

- Some interpreted them in a way that befits the linguistic usage of the Arabs.

- Some have over-interpreted them to the point that they almost tampered with their text.

- Some have made a difference between a kind of interpretation that is likely and current in the linguistic usage of the Arabs, and another kind which is far-fetched and archaic, interpreting in the former case and committing the meaning to Allah in the latter. This is reported from Malik, and among the *Khalaf* it is asserted decisively by Ibn Daqiq al-'Id (d. 702).[263]

Al-Bayhaqi said: "The safest method is to believe in them without modality, and to keep silence concerning what is meant except if the explanation is conveyed from the Prophet himself, in which case it is followed." The proof for this is the agreement of the scholars that the specific interpretation is not obligatory, and that therefore the commitment of meaning to Allah is safest....

---

[263] Ibn Hajar elsewhere reports Ibn Daqiq al-'Id's words in full: "We say concerning the various attributes that they are real and true according to the meaning Allah wills for them. As for those who interpret them, we look at their interpretation: if it is close to the rules of language in use among the Arabs we do not reject it, and if it is far from them we relinquish it and return to believing while declaring transcendence." In *Fath al-Bari* (1959 ed. 13:383).

Ibn al-'Arabi al-Maliki said:

It is reported that the innovators have rejected these hadiths, the *Salaf* passed them on as they came, and others interpreted them, and my position is the last one.[265] The saying: "He descends" refers to His acts, not His essence. Indeed, it is an expression for His angels who descend with His command and His prohibition. And just as descent can pertain to bodies, it can also pertain to ideas or spiritual notions *(ma'ânî)*. If one takes the hadith to refer to a physical occurrence, then descent would be the attribute of the angel sent to carry out an order. If one takes it to refer to a spiritual occurrence, that is, first He did not act, then He acted: this would be called a descent from one rank to another, and this is a sound Arabic meaning.

<u>In sum the hadith is interpreted in two ways: the first is: His command or His angel descends; the second is: it is a metaphor for His regard for supplicants, His answering them, and so forth.</u>

Abu Bakr ibn Furak has said that some of the masters have read it *yunzilu* – "He sends down" – instead of *yanzilu* – "He descends" – that is, He sends down an angel. This is strengthened by al-Nasa'i's narration through al-Aghurr from Abu Hurayra and Abu Sa'id al-Khudri: "Allah waits until the first part of the night is over, then He orders a herald to say: Is there anyone supplicating so that he may be answered?..."[266] There is also the hadith of 'Uthman ibn Abi al-'As: "The gates of heaven are opened in the middle of the night and a herald calls out: Is there anyone supplicating so that he may be an-

---

[265] Again Bin Baz here interjects: "This is an obvious mistake which goes against the plain import of the texts that have come to us concerning the descent, and likewise what is cited of Baydawi later is null and void. The correct position is that of the Pious *Salaf* who believed in the descent and let the texts pass as they came to them, affirming Allah's descent in the sense that befits Him, without asking how nor giving an example, just as the rest of His attributes. That is the safest, straightest, most knowledgeable, and wisest way. Therefore hold on to it, cling to it stubbornly, and beware what contravenes it so that you may reach safety. And Allah knows best." The gist of these remarks is that Bin Baz refuses to preclude displacement from Allah.

[266] See above, n. 254.

swered?..."²⁶⁶ Al-Qurtubi said: "This clears all ambiguity, and there is no interference by the narration of Rifaʻa al-Juhani whereby "Allah descends to the nearest heaven and says: I do not ask about My servants anyone besides Myself,"²⁶⁷ for there is nothing in this which precludes the above-mentioned interpretation."

Al-Baydawi said:

> Since it is established with decisive proofs that the Exalted is transcendent above having a body or being circumscribed by boundaries, it is forbidden to attribute to Him descent in the sense of displacement from one place to another place lower than it. What is meant is the light of His mercy: that is, He moves from what is pursuant to the attribute of Majesty entailing wrath and punishment, to what is pursuant to the attribute of Generosity entailing kindness and mercy."²⁶⁸

Some Misleading Reports From the *Salaf*

One of the *Jahmi* scholars said to Ishaq ibn Rahuyah: "I disbelieve in a Lord that descends from one heaven to another heaven," whereupon he replied: "I believe in a Lord that does what He wishes."²⁶⁹ This response is also narrated from Fudayl ibn ʻIyad, Yahya ibn Maʻin, and al-Awzaʻi.²⁷⁰ Al-Bayhaqi narrates the incident with a sound chain through al-Hakim from Ishaq ibn Rahuyah, and he identifies the Jahmi scholar as Ibrahim ibn Abi Salih, then comments: "Ishaq ibn Ibrahim al-Hanzali made it clear, in this report, that he considers the descent *(al-nuzûl)* one of the attributes of action *(min sifât al-fiʻl)*. Secondly, he spoke of a descent without 'how'. This proves

---

²⁶⁶See above, n. 255.
²⁶⁷Narrated from Rifaʻa ibn ʻAraba al-Juhani as part of a longer hadith by al-Darimi in his *Musnad*, Ahmad in his, al-Nasaʼi in *ʻAmal al-Yawm wa al-Layla*, Ibn Majah in his *Sunan*, al-Tabarani in *al-Kabir* (5:49-51 #4556-4558), Ibn Hibban with a sound chain in his *Sahih* according to al-Arnaʼut (1:444 #212), al-Tayalisi in his *Musnad* (p. 182 #1292), al-Bazzar in his. Al-Haythami in *Majmaʻ al-Zawaʼid* (10:408) said that some of al-Tabarani's and al-Bazzar's chains are sound.
²⁶⁸Ibn Hajar, *Fath al-Bari* (1989 ed. 3:37-38; 1959 ed. 3:32-33 #1094).
²⁶⁹Narrated by al-Dhahabi who identifies the scholar as Ibrahim ibn [Hisham] Abi Salih in *Mukhtasar al-ʻUluw* (p. 191 #234).
²⁷⁰See n. 286.

he did not hold displacement *(al-intiqâl)* and movement from one place to another *(al-zawâl)* concerning it."²⁷²

Beyond disputation or misleading concision, *Ahl al-Sunna* accept and believe all the authentic reports that came from the Prophet ﷺ, including the hadith of Allah's "descent" to the nearest heaven, and they believe, at the same time, in a Lord that does what He wishes *and* befits Him. This was elaborated by Ibn Jahbal al-Kilabi in his lengthy refutation of Ibn Taymiyya's belief on Allah's "direction" *(jiha)*, "aboveness" *(fawqiyya)*, and "descent" *(nuzûl)*.²⁷³

No doubt related to the above is Ibn Taymiyya's addition from Ibn Rahuyah whereby he said: "He is able to descend without the Throne being vacant of Him" *(yaqdiru an yanzila min ghayri an yakhlua al-'arshu minhu)*! This is identical with Hammad ibn Zayd's reported view that "He is in His place and He comes near His servants however He wishes" *(huwa fi makânihi yaqrubu min khalqihi kayfa shâ')*.²⁷⁴ Ibn Taymiyya also attributes this position to Ibn Mandah – Abu Bakr al-Najjad's student – who composed a book he named *al-Radd 'Ala Man Za'ama Anna Allaha Fi Kulli Makan Wa 'Ala Man Za'ama Anna Allaha Laysa Lahu Makan, Wa 'Ala Man Ta'awwala al-Nuzula 'Ala Ghayri al-Nuzul* ("Refutation of Those Who Claim That Allah Is In Every Place, and Of Those Who Claim That He Is Not In Any Place, and Of Those Who Interpret the Descent to Mean Other than the Descent").²⁷⁵

Al-Khattabi's Commentary

Bayhaqi follows up on the narration of Ibn Rahuyah's reply with the following explanation by Abu Sulayman al-Khattabi:

> One does not imagine of the descent of One Who is not governed by the attributes of bodies that it pertains to the meanings of a descent from top to bottom, or a displacement from above to

---

²⁷²In *al-Asma' wa al-Sifat* (2:375-376 #951),
²⁷³Its text is replicated in Ibn al-Subki's *Tabaqat* (9:35-91) and we have translated it in full in a separate publication: *The Refutation of Ibn Taymiyya's Doctrine Which Attributes a Direction to Allah.*
²⁷⁴Quoted in al-Dhahabi, *Siyar* (8:213).
²⁷⁵In *Majmu' Fatawa Ibn Taymiyya* (5:376-380).

below. It is only a report of His power and benevolence towards His creatures, His pity for them, His responsiveness to their supplications, and His forgiveness of them. He does what He wishes, modality is not applied to His attributes, nor quantity to His acts. Glory to Him! ⟨**There is nothing whatsoever like unto Him, and He is the All-Hearing, the All-Seeing.**⟩ (42:11).... The position of all the Predecessors concerning the above is just as we said, and it was narrated narrated thus from a group of the Companions.[275] One of the shaykhs among the hadith scholars who are foremost references in the knowledge of narrations and narrators slipped and turned away from this path when he narrated the hadith of descent and then remarked: 'If someone asks how our Lord descends to the heaven, the answer is: He descends as He wishes; if he asks: Does He move *(hal yataharrak)* when He descends? The answer is: If He wishes, He moves, and if He does not wish, He does not move.' And this is a gross and crucial mistake *(khata' fâhish 'azîm)*! For Allah Almighty is not described by movement, since movement and stillness follow one after the other in the same entity: it is specifically possible to attribute movement to whatever can be attributed stillness, and both of them are among the accidents of originated matter *(min a'râd al-hadath)* and the attributes of creatures. Whereas Allah is exalted high above them, ⟨**There is nothing whatsoever like unto Him.**⟩ (42:11) If that shaykh had trodden the path of the pious Predecessors and had not ventured into what is of no concern to him, he would not have come out with a statement such as this gross mistake. I only mentioned this so that such manner of talk should be cautiously avoided, for it does not result in good nor in the benefit of guidance. We ask Allah protection from misguidance, from speaking in prohibited terms, falsehood, and impossibilities.[276]

Al-Khattabi in his commentary on Abu Dawud also states:

> This [hadith] belongs to the knowledge in whose outward expression we have been ordered to believe and not seek to disclose its

---

[275] Jubayr ibn Mut'im, Abu Bakr, 'Ali, Ibn Mas'ud, 'Ubada ibn al-Samit, Rufa'a ibn 'Uraba, Jabir, 'Uthman ibn Abi al'As, Abu al-Darda', Anas, 'Amr ibn 'Abasa, Ibn 'Abbas, Umm Salama, Abu Musa al-Ash'ari, and others.
[276] As quoted by al-Bayhaqi in *al-Asma' wa al-Sifat* (2:378-379 #956).

inward sense. It is one of the many ambiguities *(mutashâbih)* which Allah has mentioned in His book.²⁷⁸

Al-Maturidi, Ibn Hazm, and Ibn 'Abd al-Wahhab

Imam Abu Mansur al-Maturidi (d. 333) said: "To suggest a place for Allah is idolatry."²⁷⁹ Similarly Ibn Hazm al-Zahiri – the declared enemy of the Ash'ari school – said: "By no means whatsoever is Allah in a place or in a time. This is the position of the vast majority of the scholars *(al-jumhur)* and ours as well, and other than this position is not permissible, for anything other than it is false."²⁸⁰ He further states:

> [Allah's descent] is an act which Allah ﷻ does in the nearest heaven pertaining to an opening for the acceptance of supplication. It refers to the fact that that hour is the likeliest time for acceptance, answer, and forgiveness for those who strive, seek forgiveness, and repent.²⁸¹

Even Sulayman ibn 'Abd Allah ibn Muhammad ibn 'Abd al-Wahhab declared as an unbeliever anyone who attributed place to Allah: "Whoever believes or says: Allah is in person *(bi dhâtihi)* in every place, or in one place, is a disbeliever *(kâfir)*."²⁸² Accordingly Hammad ibn Zayd's statement that "He is in His place and He comes near His servants however He wishes,"

---

²⁷⁸Al-Khattabi, *Ma'alim al-Sunan* (Hims ed. 5:101).
²⁷⁹Quoted in Abu Hanifa, *Kitab al-Fiqh al-Akbar bi Sharh al-Qari* (Cairo: Dar al-Kutub al-'Arabiyya al-Kubra, 1327/1909) p. 16; cf. al-Maturidi, *Sharh al-Fiqh al-Akbar* in *Majmu'at Rasa'il* (Hyderabad: Matba'at Majlis Da'irat al- Ma'arif al-Nizamiyya, 1903).
²⁸⁰In *al-Fisal fi al-Milal* (2:125).
²⁸¹As cited in al-Kawthari's marginalia on *Daf' Shubah al-Tashbih* (1998 repr. p. 50). Note that 'Uthman ibn Sa'id al-Darimi stated: "We do not concede that all actions are created.... The descent, the walking, the running *(al-harwala)*, and the establishment on the Throne and to the heaven are eternal without beginning *(qadim)*." In his *Naqd al-Jahmiyya* (Cairo, 1361/1942 p. 121) as quoted in al-Kawthari's *Maqalat* (p. 314). Ibn Hazm rejected this position in *al-Fisal* (2:124): "If the establishment on the Throne is eternal without beginning, then the Throne is eternal without beginning, and this is disbelief."
²⁸²In *al-Tawdih 'an Tawhid al-Khallaq Fi Jawab Ahl al-'Iraq* (1319/1901) p. 34. New ed.: al-Riyad: Dar Tibah, 1984.

if authentic, must be interpreted in a way to suggest other than the ascription of place, as did al-Bayhaqi with Ibn Rahuyah's answer to the *Jahmi*.[282]

Ibn 'Abd al-Barr's Controversy

Literalists often quote Ibn 'Abd al-Barr's controversial words on the hadith of descent in *al-Tamhid*:

> The hadith [of Allah's descent] provides evidence that Allah is in *(fi)* the heaven, on *('alâ)* the Throne, above *(fawq)* seven heavens, as the Congregation *(jamâ'a)* said, and this is part of their proof against the *Mu'tazila* and the *Jahmiyya*'s claim that Allah is in every place and not on the Throne....
>
> Part of the right owed Allah's Speech is that it be taken in it literal sense *('alâ haqîqatihi)*, until the Community concurs that what is meant is the metaphorical meaning, when there is no way to follow what is revealed to us from our Lord except in that way....
>
> *Istawâ* is known in the language and understood to be height *('uluw)*, rising above something, fixity in a place *(al-tamkîn)*, and settledness in it *(al-istiqrâr fîh)*.... and *istawâ* is "settledness in height" *(al-istiqrâr fî al-'uluw)*. Allah said to us: **That you may mount upon** *(tastawû)* **their backs, and may remember your Lord's favor when you mount** *(istawaytum)* **thereon** (43:13), **And it (the ship) came to rest** *(istawat)* **upon (the mount) al-Judi** (11:44), and **And when you are on board** *(istawayta)* **the ship, you and whoso is with you** (23:28).[283]

---

[282]Note that in our time Muhammad Nasir al-Din al-Albani revived the claim that Allah is in a place above the Throne which he called *al-makân al-'adamî* ("the inexistential place") in his introduction to al-Dhahabi's *Mukhtasar al-'Uluw*. He was refuted by Shaykh Hasan 'Ali al-Saqqaf in his book *Talqih al-Fuhum al-'Aliya* ("The Inculcation of Lofty Discernment").

[283]See Shaykh Nuh Keller's article "Is it permissible for a Muslim to believe that 'Allah is in the sky' in a literal sense?" as well as Appendix 5, "*Istiwâ*' is a Divine Act" (p. 87).

Ibn al-'Arabi's Refutation of Ibn 'Abd al-Barr

The above was firmly rejected by Ibn al-'Arabi in his commentary on the hadith of descent in al-Tirmidhi:

> Some ignorant people have trespassed bounds in interpreting this hadith, claiming there is proof in it that Allah "is in the Heaven, on the Throne, above the seven heavens." We say that this is a sign of tremendous ignorance.
>
> What the hadith said is "He descends to Heaven" without specifying from where He descends or how He descends. Yet they said – and their proof is, again, based on the literal sense – ❪**The Merciful established Himself over the Throne**❫ (20:4).
>
> We ask: What is the Throne in Arabic, and what is *istawâ*?
>
> They reply: As Allah said: **That you may mount upon** *(tastawû)* **their backs, and may remember your Lord's favor when you mount** *(istawaytum)* **thereon** (43:13).
>
> We say: Allah is Mighty and Higher than to have His *istiwâ'* on His Throne compared to our sitting on the backs of animals.
>
> They say: And as He said: **And it (the ship) came to rest** *(istawat)* **upon (the mount) al-Judi** (11:44).
>
> We say: Allah is Mighty and Higher than a ship that sailed and then docked and stopped.
>
> They said: And as He said: **And when you are on board** *(istawayta)* **the ship, you and whoso is with you** (23:28).
>
> We say: Allah forbid that His *istiwâ'* be similar to that of Noah and his people. Everything in the latter case is created, as it consists in *istiwâ'* with an elevation and a settling in a place involving physical contact. The entire Umma is in agreement, even before hearing the hadith of descent and the arguments of those who rejected it, that

Allah's *istiwâ'* does not involve any of those things. Therefore do not give examples from His creation for Him!...

They say: Allah said: ❨"He rules all affairs from the Heaven to the Earth❩ (32:5).

We say: This is true, but it does not provide any proof for your innovation.

They say: All the firm believers in the Oneness of Allah raise their hands to the Heavens when supplicating him, and if Musa had not said to Pharaoh: "My Lord is in the Heaven," Pharaoh would not have said: ❨O Haman... set up for me a lofty tower in order that I may survey the god of Moses❩ (28:38).

We say: You are lying about Musa ﷺ, he never said that. But your conclusion shows that you are indeed the followers of Pharaoh, who believed that the Creator lies in a certain direction, and so he desired to climb up to Him on a ladder. He congratulates you for being among his followers, and he is your imam.

They say: What about Umayya ibn Abi al-Salt who said: "Glory to Him Whom creatures are unable to know in the way He deserves to be known, Who is on His Throne, One and One Alone, Sovereign and Possessor over the Throne of Heaven, unto Whose Majesty faces are humbled and prostrate"? And he – Umayya – had read the Torah, the Bible, and the Psalms.

We say: It is just like you, in your ignorance, to cite as proof, first Pharaoh, then the discourse of a pre-Islamic Arab supported by the Torah and the Bible, which have been distorted and changed. Of all of Allah's creation the Jews are the most knowledgeable in disbelief and in likening Allah to creation.[284]

---

[284] Umayya ibn Abi al-Salt recited a funeral eulogy for the disbelievers who died at Badr and died during the siege of al-Ta'if. Ibn Hajar said in *al-Isaba* (1:133 #549): "There is no contest among the authorities in history that Umayya ibn Abi Salt died an unbeliever."

<u>What we must believe is that Allah existed and nothing existed with Him; that He created all creation, including the Throne, without becoming subject to disclosure through them, nor did a direction arise for Him because of them, nor did He acquire a location in them; that He does not become immanent, that He does not cease to be transcendent, that he does not change, and that He does not move from one state to another.</u>

Istiwâ' in the Arabic language has fifteen meanings both literal and figurative. Some of these meanings are suitable for Allah and the meaning of the verse (20:4) is derived from them. The other meanings are not accepted under any circumstances. For example, if it is taken to mean being fixed in a place *(tamakkun)*, settling *(istiqrâr)*, connecting *(ittisâl)*, or being bounded *(muhâdhât)*: then none of these are suitable for the Creator ﷻ and no-one should try to find His likeness in His creation.

One may refrain from explaining the verse, as Malik and others have said: "*Istiwâ'* is known" – he means: its lexical sense– "and its modality is unknown" *(wa al-kayfu majhûl)* [286] – that is: the modality of whatever is suitable for Allah among the senses of *istiwâ'*: therefore who can specify such modality? – "and asking about it is

---

[286] This wording is not established as authentic. The sound versions are as follows: (1) "The 'how' of it is inconceivable; the 'establishment' part of it is not unknown; belief in it is obligatory; asking about it is an innovation; and I believe that you are a man of innovation." Narrated from Ja'far ibn 'Abd Allah by al-Dhahabi, *Siyar* (7:415). (2) "❬The Merciful established Himself over the Throne❭ just as He described Himself. One cannot ask 'how.' 'How' does not apply to Him. And you are an evil man, a man of innovation. Take him out!" Narrated from Ibn Wahb by al-Bayhaqi with a sound chain in *al-Asma' wa al-Sifat* (2:304-305 #866), al-Dhahabi in the *Siyar* (7:416), and Ibn Hajar in *Fath al-Bari* (1959 ed. 13:406-407; 1989 ed. 13:501). (3) "The establishment is not unknown; the "how" is inconceivable; belief in it is obligatory; asking about it is an innovation; and I do not think that you are anything but an innovator." Narrated from Yahya ibn Yahya al-Tamimi and Malik's shaykh Rabi'a ibn Abi 'Abd al-Rahman by al-Bayhaqi with a sound chain in *al-Asma' wa al-Sifat* (2:305-306 #867) and by Ibn Abi Zayd al-Qayrawani in *al-Jami' fi al-Sunan* (p. 123). Note that the wording that says: "The 'how' is unknown" *(al-kayfu majhûl)* is also narrated from Rabi'a by al-Bayhaqi in *al-Asma' wa al-Sifat* (2:306 #868) with a sound chain, but is an aberrant narration *(riwâya shâdhdha)*. Yet it is the preferred wording of Ibn Taymiyya in *Dar' Ta'arud al-'Aql wa al-Naql* (1:278) and *Majmu'a al-Fatawa* (17:373) as he infers from it support for his positions.

innovation" – because, as we have just made clear, probing this matter is looking for dubious matters and that is asking for *fitna*.

Hence, from what the Imam of Muslims Malik has said, we can conclude that the *istiwâ'* is known; that what is suitable for Allah is left unspecified; and that He is declared transcendent above what is impossible for Him. As for specifying what is not suitable for Him, it is not permissible for you, since you have completed the declaration of oneness and belief by negating likeness for Allah and by negating whatever it is absurd to believe concerning Him. There is no need for anything beyond that, and we have already explained this in detail.

As for the phrases: "He descends, He comes, He arrives," and similar ones whose meanings it is impermissible to apply to His Essence: they refer to His actions... Al-Awzaʿi explained this when he said, about this hadith: "Allah does what he wishes."[286] It suffices to know or simply to believe that Allah is not to be defined by any of the characteristics of creatures and that there is nothing in His creation that resembles Him and no interpretation that can explain Him.

They said: We must say "He descends" without asking how. We say: We seek refuge in Allah from asking how! We only say whatever Allah's Messenger ﷺ has taught us to say and what we have understood from the Arabic language in which the Qur'an was revealed. And the Prophet said: "Allah says: O My servant, I was ailing and you did not visit me, I was hungry and you did not feed me, I was thirsty and you did not give me drink..."[287] None of this is suitable of Allah whatsoever, but He has honored all these actions by expressing them through Him. In the same way, the saying "Our Lord descends" expresses that His servant and angel descends in His name with His order pertaining to whatever He bestows of His Mercy, gives out of His generosity, and showers His creation out of His bounty.

---

[286] Also related from Ishaq ibn Rahuyah as narrated by al-Bayhaqi in *al-Asma' wa al-Sifat* (2:375-376 #951) and al-Dhahabi in *Mukhtasar al-ʿUluw* (p. 191 #234) and the *Siyar* (9:558 #1877); Fudayl ibn ʿIyad as related from al-Athram by Bukhari in *Khalq Afʿal al-ʿIbad* (p. 14); Yahya ibn Maʿin as cited by Lalikaʾi in *Sharh Usul Iʿtiqad Ahl al-Sunna*. The latter two are cited by Ibn Taymiyya in *Majmuʿa al-Fatawa* (5:377).
[287] Narrated from Abu Hurayra by Muslim and Ahmad.

The poet says:

> *I have descended*
> *– therefore do not suspect me of jealousy! –*
> *in the station of the generous lover.*[289]

A descent can be either figurative or physical. The descending that Allah spoke about, if understood as physical, would mean His angel, Messenger, and slave. However, if you can understand it to mean that He was not doing any of this and that He then turned to do it in the last third of the night, thereby answering prayers, forgiving, bestowing, and that He has named this "descending from one degree to another and from one attribute to another," then that – ironically – is addressed to those who have more knowledge than you and more intelligence, who are firmer in belief in Allah's Unity and are less confused than you – nay, who are not confused at all!

They say in ignorance that if He meant the descending of his Mercy he would not make that only in the last third of the night, because His Mercy descends day and night. We say: Yes, he singled out the night, and the day of 'Arafa, and the hour of *Jum'a*, because the descent of His mercy in them is more abundant, and its bestowal is even greater then. Allah told us of this when He said: ❪**And those who beg forgiveness in the early hours of the morning**❫ (3:17).[290]

Al-'Iraqi and Ibn Jahbal's Dismissal of Ibn 'Abd al-Barr

The Renewer of the eighth Islamic century and teacher of Ibn Hajar, Shaykh al-Islam Zayn al-Din al-'Iraqi said about Ibn 'Abd al-Barr: "He is one of those who hold that Allah has a direction, therefore beware of him."[291] The Shafi'i imam Ibn Jahbal al-Kilabi indicated Ibn 'Abd al-Barr's isolation from the position of most scholars, particularly Malikis, on the questions of *istiwâ'* and descent:

---

[289]The scholars also often quote al-Shafi'i's saying that when he first arrived in Egypt they did not understand him, whereupon "I descended, and descended, and descended until they understood me."
[290]Ibn al-'Arabi, *Arida al-Ahwadhi* (2:234-237).
[291]In *Tarh al-Tathrib* (2:382).

Concerning what Abu 'Umar ibn 'Abd al-Barr said, both the elite and the general public know the man's position and the scholars' disavowal of if. The Malikis' condemnation of it, from the first to the last of them, is well-known. His contravention *(mukhâlafa)* of the Imam of North Africa, Abu al-Walid al-Baji, is famous. It reached a point that the eminent people of North Africa would say: 'No-one in North Africa holds this position except he and Ibn Abi Zayd!' although some of the people of knowledge cited an excuse for Ibn Abi Zayd in the text of the great qadi Abu Muhammad 'Abd al-Wahhab [ibn 'Ali ibn Nasr al-Baghdadi (d. 422)] al-Baghdadi al-Maliki[291] – may Allah have mercy on him.[292]

Al-Qari's Recapitulation

Al-Qari commented the following on the hadith of descent:

"Our Lord descends" means that His command descends to one or more of His angels, or that His herald descends.

"Blessed and Exalted is He" means: Abundant are His goodness, Mercy, and the marks of His beauty. Also, He is exalted above the attributes of creatures pertaining to ascent and descent, and elevated with His splendor, magnificence, and majesty above the properties of contingence. It was said that "Blessed and Exalted" are parenthetical clauses inserted between the verb and its circumstancial modifier [of time, place, etc.] to warn about transcendence, so that no-one falsely imagine that the attribution of the modifier to the verb is real.

"Every night to the lowest heaven": Ibn Hajar said: "Meaning His order and mercy descend, or His angels."[293] This is the figurative interpretation of Imam Malik[294] and others; it is indicated by the sound narration: "Allah waits until the first part of the night is over, then He

---

[291]Perhaps a reference to his commentary on Ibn Abi Zayd's *Risala* (Ibn Farhun, *Dibaj* p. 262).
[292]In Ibn al-Subki, *Tabaqat al-Shafi'iyya al-Kubra* (9:78).
[293]In *Fath al-Bari* (1959 ed. 3:32 #1094), as quoted above, in the underlined passage.
[294]See n. 256.

orders a herald *(munâdiyan)* to say: Is there anyone supplicating so that he may be answered, etc."²⁹⁶ A second figurative interpretation – also attributed to Imam Malik – is that it is a metaphor *(isti'âra)* to signify turning to *(iqbâl)* ²⁹⁷ the supplicant with fulfillment, kindness, mercy, and the acceptance of remorse in the manner of the generous, especially kings when they alight near the needy and weak.

Al-Nawawi said in *Sharh Muslim*:

> There are, concerning this hadith and those like it among the hadiths and verses of the divine Attributes, two well-known schools of thought. The school of the vast majority of the *Salaf* and some of the sholars of *kalâm* holds that we must believe in their reality according to what befits Allah ﷻ, but that the literal import we commonly apply to ourselves is not meant, nor do we say anything to interpret them figuratively, believing firmly that Allah is utterly transcendent above the properties of contingence *(hudûth)*.²⁹⁸ The second school is that of the majority of the scholars of *kalâm* and a number of the *Salaf* – related from Malik and al-Awza'i – and holds that they are interpreted figuratively but only according to their appropriate contextual meanings. On that basis, this hadith has two interpretations.²⁹⁹

Then he cited the two interpretations we mentioned above. From what he said, as well as from the words of the godly scholar Abu Ishaq al-Shirazi, Imam al-Haramayn, al-Ghazali, and others both among our own Imams and the rest, it is understood that the two schools agree upon the dismissal of the literal meaning of the following: the "coming" *(al-majî')*, the "form" *(al-sûra)*, the "person" *(al-shakhs)*, the "leg" *(al-rijl)*, the "foot" *(al-qidam)*, the "hand" *(al-yad)*, the "face" *(al-wajh)*, "anger" *(al-ghadab)*, "mercy" *(al-rahma)*, the "establishment over the Throne" *(al-istiwâ' 'alâ al-'arsh)*, the "being in the heaven" *(al-kawn fî al-samâ')*, and others. Understood literally, all these would necessarily result in definitely false impossibilities entailing

---

²⁹⁶See n. 254.
²⁹⁷Attributed to Hammad ibn Zayd by al-Bayhaqi (*AS* p. 456, *ASH* 2:380) as stated.
²⁹⁸Note the strong affirmation of both the reality of the Attributes and Allah's transcendence which is the mark of the accomplished scolars of *Ahl al-Sunna* in doctrine.
²⁹⁹Al-Nawawi, *Sharh Sahih Muslim*, Book of *Salat al-Musafirin wa Qasruha*.

positions whose status is disbelief *(kufr)* by Consensus. Due to this, all of the *Khalaf* and *Salaf* were compelled to dismiss the literal meaning of the word.

They differed only with regard to the following: Should we dismiss the literal meaning while believing firmly that Allah ﷻ described Himself with whatever befits His majesty and magnificence, without interpreting it figuratively as something else? This is the way of most of the *Salaf*, and it involves a non-specific type of figurative interpretation *(ta'wîl ijmâlî)*. Or should we dismiss the literal meaning while believing firmly that Allah ﷻ described Himself with whatever befits His majesty and magnificence, and interpreting it figuratively as something else? This is the way of most of the *Khalaf*, and it consists in a specific type of figurative interpretation *(ta'wîl tafsîlî)*.[299]

The *Khalaf* did not want, in adopting the latter, to deliberately contravene the pious *Salaf* – we seek refuge in Allah from such a notion about them! However, it was only out of the necessity in which their times placed them, because of the abundance of the *mujassima* and *Jahmiyya* among other misguided sects, and their sway over the minds of the general public. By adopting specific figurative interpretation, they aimed to deter them and prove their doctrines false. Thereafter, many of them expressed regret and said: "If we had the pious *Salaf*'s purity of doctrine and enjoyed the scarcity of naysayers which they enjoyed in their time, we would not probe into the figurative interpretation of any of these."

It is by now clear that Malik and al-Awza'i – major figures of the *Salaf* – interpreted this hadith in its specifics. Similarly did Sufyan al-Thawri interpret *istiwâ'* over the Throne as the decision of Allah's command, its equivalent being ⟨**Then turned He** *(thumma istawâ)* **to the heaven when it was smoke**⟩ (41:11).[300] Among those who did the

---

[299] See al-Buti's excellent discussion of these two types in *al-Salafiyya* (p. 132-144), translated in Shaykh Hisham Kabbani's *Islamic Beliefs and Doctrine According to Ahl al-Sunna* and his *Encyclopedia of Islamic Knowledge*.
[300] "The understanding of *istiwâ'* as Allah's turning to a particular command concerning the Throne is not far-fetched, and this is the *ta'wîl* of Imam Sufyan al-Thawri, who took as corroborating evidence for it the verse: ⟨**Then turned He to the heaven when it was smoke**⟩ (41:11), meaning: "He proceeded to it" *(qasada ilayhâ)*." In al-Yafi'i, *Marham al-'Ilal* (p. 245) and Abu al-Ma'ali al-Juwayni, *al-Irshad* (p. 59-60).

same is Imam Ja'far al-Sadiq. Indeed a whole group of them, as well as later scholars, said that whoever believes Allah to be in a particular physical direction is an unbeliever, as al-'Iraqi has explicitly stated, saying:

> This is the position of Abu Hanifa, Malik, al-Shafi'i, al-Ash'ari, and al-Baqillani. All the groups have agreed upon interpreting such texts as ❪And He is with you wheresoever you may be❫ (57:4), ❪There is no secret conference of three but He is their fourth[, nor of five but He is their sixth, nor of less than that or more but He is with them wheresoever they may be]❫ (58:7), ❪Wheresoever you turn, there is Allah's countenance❫ (2:115), ❪We are nearer to him than his jugular vein❫ (50:16), "There is no heart except it lies between the two fingers of the Merciful,"[301] and "The Black Stone is Allah's right hand on earth."[302] This agreement makes plain to the reader the validity of the authorities' decision that the pause in the verse
>
> ❪None knows its explanation *(ta'wîl)* save Allah
> And those who are firmly grounded in knowledge
> [They] say: We believe therein❫[303] (3:7)
>
> is after the clause "who are firmly grounded in knowledge," not Allah's name.[304]

---

[301] See n. 85.
[302] See n. 48.
[303] On the various positions on this question, see Ibn Kathir's *Tafsir* for this verse and especially al-Dani's (d. 444) *al-Muktafa fi al-Waqf wa al-Ibtida'*.
[304] As al-Qari goes on to say the majority stop at Allah's name, but both readings are possible, as stated by al-Suyuti in *al-Itqan* (1:264), al-Raghib in *Mufradat Alfaz al-Qur'an*, and al-Dani in *al-Muktafa* (p. 195-197). The Prophet ﷺ defined ❪those who are firmly grounded in knowledge❫ (3:7) as "Those whose oaths are kept, whose tongues are truthful, whose hearts are upright, and whose stomachs and genitals are abstinent. They are among ❪those who are firmly grounded in knowledge❫." Narrated from Abu al-Darda', Abu Umama, Wathila, and Anas by al-Tabarani in *al-Kabir* (8:152 #7658), and from Ibn 'Abbas by al-Hakim ('Ata' ed. 8:152 #7658) with a sound chain as confirmed by al-Dhahabi.

I say: The vast majority consider that the pause comes at Allah's name, and have declared it a mandatory pause *(waqf lâzim)*. This is the literal meaning, for *ta'wîl* is the meaning which Allah ﷻ meant, and in reality none knows that meaning except Allah ﷻ, and there is no God beside Him. One that speaks concerning its meaning is speaking only according to what is shown to him, and no-one can say: "This interpretation is what Allah meant" categorically.

The disagreement, in the final analysis, is verbal. Hence, many of the latter-day authoritative scholars have avoided designating the interpretation *(ta'yîn al-ta'wîl)* as any given item among the suitable items of a word, leaving its designation to Allah's knowledge. This is a median position between the two schools and a pleasing taste of the two springs. Ibn Daqiq al-'Id chose another median position, saying:

> If interpretation stems from an evident and prevalent figurative understanding, then it ought to be applied without reserve. If it stems from a far-fetched, aberrant figurative understanding, then it ought to be left out. If one is as good as the other, then difference in its permissibility or impermissibility is a matter of juridical effort. This matter does not present any danger to the two sides of the argument.

I say: Reserving judgment in this matter is only for lack of a preponderant alternative, although reserving judgment is supported by the position of the *Salaf*, among them the Greatest Imam [Abu Hanifa], and Allah knows best.

Al-Qadi ['Iyad] said:

> What is meant by His descent is the approach of His Mercy, the increase of His kindness toward His servants, and the acceptance of their contrition, in the custom of generous kings and clement liege-lords when they alight near a needy, suffering and weak people.

It was narrated: "Allah comes down from the highest heaven to the lowest heaven."[306] That is: He shifts from all that is necessitated by the Attributes of Majesty – such as the rejection of the arrogant, indifference to them, the subduing of enemies, and the exacting of punishment from the wicked – to all that is necessitated by the Attributes of Beauty, such as forbearance, mercy, the acceptance of contrition, gentleness toward the destitute, fulfillment of needs, leniency and alleviation in the commands and prohibitions, and pardon towards apparent sins. Hence it was said that this is a figural manifestation *(tajallî sûrî)* and not a real descent *(nuzûl haqîqî)*. The difficulty is thereby resolved, and Allah knows best.[307]

---

[306]Narrated from Abu al-Khattab by al-Tabarani in *al-Kabir* (22:370 #927) with a weak chain as indicated by al-Haythami in *Majma' al-Zawa'id*.
[307]Al-Qari, *Mirqat al-Mafatih* (1892 ed. 2:136-137, 1994 ed. 3:298-301).

BIBLIOGRAPHY

'Abd al-Qahir al-Baghdadi. *Usul al-Din*. Istanbul: Dar al-Funun fi Madrasa al-Ilahiyyat, 1928.

Abu Nu'aym al-Asfahani. *Hilya al-Awliya' wa Tabaqat al-Asfiya'*. 12 vols. Ed. Mustafa 'Abd al-Qadir 'Ata. Beirut: Dar al-Kutub al-'Ilmiyya, 1997.

Abu Ya'la al-Musili. *Musnad*. 13 vols. Ed. Husayn Salim Asad. Damascus: Dar al-Ma'mun li al-Turath, 1984.

Al-Ahdab, Khaldun. *Zawa'id Tarikh Baghdad 'Ala al-Kutub al-Sitta*. 10 vols. Damascus: Dar al-Qalam, 1996.

Ahmad ibn Hanbal. *Al-'Ilal wa Ma'rifa al-Rijal*. 4 vols. Ed. Wasi Allah ibn Muhammad 'Abbas. Beirut and Riyadh: al-Maktab al-Islami, 1988.

-------. *Al-Musnad*. 20 vols. Ed. Ahmad Shakir and Hamza Ahmad al-Zayn. Cairo: Dar al-Hadith, 1995.

Al-Bayhaqi, Abu Bakr. *Al-Asma' wa al-Sifat*. Ed. Muhammad Zahid al-Kawthari. Beirut: Dar Ihya' al-Turath al-'Arabi, n.d. Reprint of the 1358/1939 Cairo edition.

-------. *Al-Asma' wa al-Sifat*. 2 vols. Ed. 'Abd Allah al-Hashidi. Riyad: Maktaba al-Sawadi, 1993.

Al-Bukhari. *Khalq Af'al al-'Ibad*. Beirut: Mu'assasa al-Risala, 1990.

Al-Buti, Muhammad Sa'id Ramadan. *Kubra al-Yaqinat al-Kawniyya*. Beirut and Damascus: Dar al-Fikr, 1997.

-------. *Al-Salafiyya Marhalatun Zamaniyyatun Mubaraka La Madhhabun Islami*. Damascus: Dar al-Fikr, 1988.

Al-Dani al-Andalusi, Abu 'Amr 'Uthman ibn Sa'id. *Al-Muktafa fi al-Waqf wa al-Ibtida'*. 2nd ed. Ed. Yusuf 'Abd al-Rahman al-Mar'ashli. Beirut: Mu'assasa al-Risala, 1987.

Al-Darimi. *Musnad*. 2 vols. Ed. Fu'ad Ahmad Zamarli and Khalid al-Sab' al-'Ilmi. Beirut: Dar al-Kitab al-'Arabi, 1987.

Al-Darqash, al-Hadi. *Abu Muhammad 'Abd Allah ibn Abi Zayd al-Qayrawani, Hayatuh wa Atharuh*. Beirut and Damascus: Dar Qutayba, 1989.

Al-Dhahabi. *Mizan al-I'tidal*. 4 vols. Ed. 'Ali Muhammad al-Bajawi. Beirut: Dar al-Ma'rifa, 1963.

-------. *Mukhtasar al-'Uluw li al-'Ali al-Ghaffar*. Ed. M. Nasir al-Din al-Albani. Beirut: al-Maktab al-Islami, 1991^2.

-------. *Siyar A'lam al-Nubala'*. 19 vols. Ed. Muhibb al-Din al-'Amrawi. Beirut: Dar al-Fikr, 1996.

-------. *Tadhkira al-Huffaz*. 4 vols. in 2. Ed. 'Abd al-Rahman ibn Yahya al-Mu'allimi. A fifth volume, titled *Dhayl Tadhkira al-Huffaz*, consists in al-Husayni's *Dhayl Tadhkira al-Huffaz*, Muhammad ibn Fahd al-Makki's *Lahz al-Alhaz bi Dhayl*

Tadhkira al-Huffaz, and al-Suyuti's *Dhayl Tabaqat al-Huffaz*. Ed. Muhammad Zahid al-Kawthari. Beirut: Dar Ihya' al-Turath al-'Arabi and Dar al-Kutub al-'Ilmiyya, n.d. Reprint of the 1968 Hyderabad edition.

Al-Hakim. *Al-Mustadrak 'Ala al-Sahihayn*. With al-Dhahabi's *Talkhis al-Mustadrak*. 5 vols. Indexes by Yusuf 'Abd al-Rahman al-Mar'ashli. Beirut: Dar al-Ma'rifa, 1986.

-------. *Al-Mustadrak 'Ala al-Sahihayn*. With al-Dhahabi's *Talkhis al-Mustadrak*. 4 vols. Annotations by Mustafa 'Abd al-Qadir 'Ata'. Beirut: Dar al-Kutub al-'Ilmiyya, 1990.

Al-Haytami, Ahmad. *Al-Khayrat al-Hisan fi Manaqib Abi Hanifa al-Nu'man*. Cairo: al-Halabi, 1326/1908.

Al-Haythami, Nur al-Din. *Majma' al-Zawa'id wa Manba' al-Fawa'id*. 3rd ed. 10 vols. Beirut: Dar al-Kitab al-'Arabi, 1982.

Ibn 'Abd al-Salam. *Fatawa*. Ed. 'Abd al-Rahman ibn 'Abd al-Fattah. Beirut: Dar al-Ma'rifa, 1986.

Ibn Abi 'Asim. *Al-Sunna*. Ed. M. Nasir al-Din al-Albani. Beirut and Damascus: Al-Maktab al-Islami, 1993.

Ibn Abi Ya'la. *Tabaqat al-Hanabila*. 2 vols. Ed. Muhammad Hamid al-Fiqqi. Cairo: Dar Ihya' al-Kutub al-'Arabiyya, n.d.

Ibn Abi Zayd al-Qayrawani. *Al-Jami' fi al-Sunan wa al-Adab wa al-Maghazi wa al-Tarikh*. Ed. M. Abu al-Ajfan and 'Uthman Battikh. Beirut: Mu'assasa al-Risala; Tunis: al-Maktaba al-'Atiqa, 1982.

Ibn al-'Arabi, Abu Bakr. *'Arida al-Ahwadhi Sharh Sunan al-Tirmidhi*. 13 vols. Beirut, Dar al-Kutub al-'Ilmiyya, n.d.

Ibn 'Asakir. *Tabyin Kadhib al-Muftari Fi Ma Nasaba ila al-Imam Abi al-Hasan al-Ash'ari*. Ed. Ahmad Hijazi al-Saqqa. Beirut: Dar al-Jil, 1995.

Ibn al-Athir. *Al-Nihaya fi Gharib al-Athar*. 5 vols. Eds. Tahir Ahmad al-Zawi and Mahmud Muhammad al-Tabbakhi. Beirut: Dar al-Fikr, 1979.

Ibn Farhun. *Al-Dibaj al-Mudhahhab fi Ma'rifa 'Ulama' al-Madhhab*. Ed. Ma'mun ibn Muhyi al-Din al-Jannan. Beirut: Dar al-Kutub al-'Ilmiyya, 1996.

Ibn Hajar. *Fath al-Bari Sharh Sahih al-Bhari*. 14 vols. Notes by 'Abd al-'Aziz ibn Baz. Beirut: Dar al-Kutub al-'Ilmiyya, 1989. Includes al-Bukhari's *Sahih*.

-------. *Ibidem*. 13 vols. Ed. Muhammad Fouad 'Abd al-Baqi and Muhibb al-Din al-Khatib. Beirut: Dar al-Ma'rifa, 1959.

-------. *Al-Isaba fi Tamyiz al-Sahaba*. 8 vols. Calcutta, 1853.

Ibn Hibban. *Sahih Ibn Hibban bi Tartib Ibn Balban*. 18 vols. Ed. Shu'ayb al-Arna'ut. Beirut: Mu'assasa al-Risala, 1993.

Ibn al-Jawzi. *Daf' Shubah al-Tashbih bi Akuff al-Tanzih*. Ed. Hasan 'Ali al-Saqqaf. Amman: Dar al-Imam Nawawi, 1991.

-------. *Daf' Shubah al-Tashbih bi Akuff al-Tanzih*. Ed. Muhammad Zahid al-Kawthari. Reprint Cairo: al-Maktaba al-Azhariyya li al-Turath, 1998.

-------. *Manaqib al-Imam Ahmad*. 2nd ed. Ed. Muhammad Amin al-Khanji al-Kutbi. Beirut: Khanji wa Hamdan, 1349/1930-1931.

Ibn Majah. *Sunan.* See al-Suyuti *et al.*, *Sharh Sunan Ibn Majah.*
Ibn Qayyim al-Jawziyya. *Bada'i' al-Fawa'id.* 4 vols. in 2. Cairo: al-Matba'a al-Muniriya, 1900?
-------. *Bada'i' al-Fawa'id.* 2 vols. Ed. Bashshar 'Uyun. Damascus: Maktaba Dar al-Bayan, 1994.
-------. *Zad al-Ma'ad fi Hadi Khayr al-'Ibad.* 6 vols. Eds. 'Abd al-Qadir al-Arna'ut and Shu'ayb al-Arna'ut. Beirut: Mu'assasa al-Risala, 1997.
Ibn Qudama, Muwaffaq al-Din. *Lam'a al-I'tiqad.* Ed. 'Abd al-Qadir Badran and Bashir Muhammad 'Uyun. Damascus: Dar al-Bayan, 1992.
Ibn Qutayba. *Ta'wil Mukhtalaf al-Hadith.* Ed. Muhammad Zuhri al-Najjar. Beirut: Dar al-Jil, 1972.
Ibn Rajab. *Dhayl Tabaqat al-Hanabila.* 2 vols. Ed. Muhammad Hamid al-Fiqqi. Cairo: Dar Ihya' al-Kutub al-'Arabiyya, n.d.
Ibn Sallam. *Gharib al-Hadith.* 2 vols. Beirut: Dar al-Kitab al-'Arabi, 1976; Dar al-Kutub al-'Ilmiyya, 1986. Neither edition mentions the editor.
Ibn al-Subki. *Qa'ida fi al-Jarh wa al-Ta'dil.* Ed. 'Abd al-Fattah Abu Ghudda. 2nd ed. Cairo, 1978. 5th ed. Aleppo & Beirut: Maktab al-Matbu'at al-Islamiyya, 1984.
-------. *Tabaqat al-Shafi'iyya al-Kubra.* 10 vols. Ed. Mahmud M. al-Tannahi and 'Abd al-Fattah M. al-Hilw. 2nd. ed. Jiza: Dar Hijr, 1992.
Ibn Taymiyya. *Majmu' Fatawa Ibn Taymiyya.* 36 vols. Cairo, 1984.
Al-'Iraqi. *Tarh al-Tathrib fi Sharh al-Taqrib.* 8 vols. in 4. Ed. Mahmud Hasan Rabi'. Beirut: Dar Ihya' al-Turath al-'Arabi, 1992. Repr. of the Cairo edition.
Al-Juwayni, Imam al-Haramayn. *Al-Irshad ila Qawati' al-Adilla fi Usul al-I'tiqad.* Ed. As'ad Tamim. Beirut: Mu'assasa al-Kutub al-Thaqafiyya, 1996.
Kabbani, Shaykh Muhammad Hisham. *Encyclopedia of Islamic Doctrine.* 7 vols. Moutain View: Al-Sunna Foundation of America, 1998.
-------. *Islamic Beliefs and Doctrine According to Ahl al-Sunna.* Vol. 1. Mountain View: Al-Sunna Foundation of America, 1996.
Al-Kattani, al-Sayyid Muhammad ibn Ja'far. *Nazm al-Mutanathir fi al-Hadith al-Mutawatir.* Beirut: Dar al-Kutub al-'Ilmiyya, 1980.
Lahmar, Hamid. *Al-Imam Malik Mufassiran.* Beirut: Dar al-Fikr, 1995.
Ma'ruf, Bashshar 'Awwad. *Al-Dhahabi wa Minhajuhu fi Kitabihi Tarikh al-Islam.* Cairo: 'Isa al-Babi al-Halabi, 1976.
Al-Mubarakfuri. *Tuhfa al-Ahwadhi bi Sharh Jami' al-Tirmidhi.* 10 vols. Beirut: Dar al-Kutub al-'Ilmiyya, 1990. Includes al-Tirmidhi's *Sunan.*
Al Munawi. *Fayd al-Qadir.* 2nd ed. 6 vols. Beirut: Dar al Ma'rifa, 1972.
Muslim. *Sahih.* See al-Nawawi, *Sharh Sahih Muslim.*
Al-Nasa'i. *'Amal al-Yawm wa al-Layla.* 2nd ed. Ed. Faruq Hammada. Beirut: Mu'assasa al-Risala, 1986.
-------. *Sunan.* See al-Suyuti, *Sharh Sunan al-Nasa'i.*
-------. *Al-Sunan al-Kubra.* 6 vols. Eds. 'Abd al-Ghaffar Sulayman al-Bandari and Sayyid Kisrawi Hasan. Beirut: Dar al-Kutub al-'Ilmiyya, 1991.

Al-Nawawi. *Sharh Sahih Muslim*. 18 vols. Ed. Khalil al-Mays. Beirut: Dar al-Kutub al-'Ilmiyya, n.d. Includes Muslim's *Sahih*.

Al-Qari. *Al-Asrar al-Marfu'a fi al-Ahadith al-Mawdu'a. (Al-Mawdu'at al-Kubra)*. 2nd ed. Ed. Muhammad ibn Lutfi al-Sabbagh. Beirut and Damascus: al-Maktab al-Islami, 1986. [1st ed. 1971.]

-------. *Mirqat al-Mafatih Sharh Mishkat al-Masabih*. 5 vols. Ed. Muhammad al-Zuhri al-Ghamrawi. Cairo: al-Matba'a al-Maymuniyya, 1309/1892 Reprint Beirut: Dar Ihya' al-Turath al-'Arabi, n.d.

-------. *Mirqat al-Mafatih Sharh Mishkat al-Masabih*. Together with Ibn Hajar's *Ajwiba 'Ala Risala al-Qazwini Hawla Ba'd Ahadith al-Masabih*. 11 vols. Ed. Sidqi Muhammad Jamil al-'Attar. Damascus: Dar al-Fikr, 1994.

Al-Qurtubi. *Al-Jami' li Ahkam al-Qur'an*. 2nd ed. 14 vols. Beirut: Dar Ihya' al-Turath al- 'Arabi, 1952. Reprint.

Al-Saqqaf, Hasan 'Ali. *Aqwal al-Huffaz al-Manthura li Bayan Wad' Hadith Ra'aytu Rabbi fi Ahsani Sura*. Amman: Dar al-Imam al-Nawawi.

-------. *Talqih al-Fuhum al-'Aliya*. Amman: Dar al-Imam al-Nawawi.

Shatta, Ibrahim al-Dusuqi. *Sira al-Shaykh al-Kabir Abi 'Abd Allah Muhammad ibn Khafif al-Shirazi*. Cairo: al-Hay'a al-'Amma li Shu'un al-Matabi' al-Amiriyya, 1977.

Al-Suyuti. *Al-Itqan fi 'Ulum al-Qur'an*. 2 vols. Ed. Mustafa Dib al-Bugha. Damascus: Dar Ibn Kathir, 1993.

-------. *Sharh Sunan al-Nasa'i*. 9 vols. Ed. 'Abd al-Fattah Abu Ghudda. Aleppo & Beirut: Maktab al-Matbu'at al-Islamiyya, 1986. Includes al-Nasa'is' *Sunan*.

-------, 'Abd al-Ghani al-Dihlawi, and Fakhr al-Hasan al-Gangohi. *Sharh Sunan Ibn Majah*. Karachi: Qadimi Kutub Khana, n.d. Includes Ibn Majah's *Sunan*.

Al-Tabarani. *Al-Mu'jam al-Kabir*. 20 vols. Ed. Hamdi ibn 'Abd al-Majid al-Salafi. Mosul: Maktaba al-'Ulum wa al-Hikam, 1983.

Al-Tahawi. *Mushkil al-Athar*. Hyderabad: Da'ira al-Ma'arif al-'Uthmaniyya, 1915.

Al-Tirmidhi. *Sunan*. See al-Mubarakfuri, *Tuhfa al-Ahwadhi*.

Al-Wahidi. *Asbab al-Nuzul*. Ed. Ayman Salih Sha'ban. Cairo: Dar al-Hadith, 1996.

Al-Yafi'i. *Marham al-'Ilal al-Mu'dila fi Daf' al-Shubah wa al-Radd 'ala al-Mu'tazila*. Ed. E. Denison Ross. Calcutta: Asiatic Society of Bengal, 1910.